Enhancing Sexuality

A Problem-Solving Approach

Client Workbook

John P. Wincze
David H. Barlow

TherapyWorks
From The Psychological Corporation

Contents

Comments About the Program

"*Enhancing Sexuality: A Problem-Solving Approach* presents a comprehensive program developed by psychologists who are not only experts in the treatment of sexual problems but leaders in the field. It is based on solid research and written in a way that may be understood by the lay person. By exploring the development of sexual behavior and ways of reacting to sexual problems, the authors give the reader a deeper understanding of the psychological, medical, and social factors that affect sexuality. This insightful workbook combines case studies with good, practical advice. The nonjudgmental and supportive attitudes of the authors are reflected in their sensitivity to cultural diversity and sexual preference. This volume is a worthy addition to the library of both patient and therapist. I plan to recommend it often."

Carol Landau, PhD
Clinical Professor of Psychiatry and Human Behavior
Director of Psychological Services, Women's Health Associates
Rhode Island Hospital and Brown University School of Medicine
Author, *The Complete Book of Menopause: Woman's Guide to Good Health*

"This excellent patient Workbook provides a no-nonsense, up-to-date approach to sexual enhancement for men and women of all ages. This Workbook covers a wide gamut of sexual difficulties and problems, and offers information, advice, and practical suggestions for every problem. A major strength of the Workbook is the large number of self-test exercises and assignments throughout. These help greatly to maintain the reader's interest and involvement. Another major strength is the balanced presentation of physical and psychological causes of sexual dysfunction. At a time when most popular literature is focusing on physical causes, this Workbook succeeds in giving the reader a truly balanced overview of the subject. The coverage is both complete and very readable. Case studies are presented throughout, and provide excellent illustrations of the main points. Finally, the first author (John Wincze) is a world-renowned clinician and researcher in the field of human sexuality who writes with exceptional clarity and comfort on the topic. This is a highly readable and authoritative Workbook on sexual enhancement, which should be read by anyone with sexual concerns or difficulties."

Raymond C. Rosen, PhD
Professor of Psychiatry
Center for Sexual and Marital Health
UMDNJ, New Jersey's University of the Health Sciences
Robert Wood Johnson Medical School

About the Authors

JOHN P. WINCZE received his PhD from the University of Vermont in 1970, and has published three books and more than 50 articles and chapters, mostly in the area of sexual problems. Recent works include *Sexual Dysfunction: A Guide for Assessment and Treatment* (1991) coauthored by Michael Carey; "Assessment and Treatment of Atypical Sexual Behavior" (*Principles and Practice of Sex Therapy*, Leiblum and Rosen, Eds., 1989); "Marital Discord and Sexual Dysfunction Associated With a Male Partner's Sexual Addiction" (*Case Studies in Sex Therapy*, Leiblum and Rosen, Eds., 1995).

Formerly, Dr. Wincze was an associate professor of psychology at Dalhousie University, Halifax, Nova Scotia. Currently, he is a professor in the Department of Psychiatry and Human Behavior and the Department of Psychology, Brown University. He is also the Chair of the Licensing Board in Psychology for the State of Rhode Island.

DAVID H. BARLOW received his PhD from the University of Vermont in 1969, and he has published 15 books and more than 200 articles and chapters, mostly in the areas of anxiety disorders, sexual problems, and clinical research methodology. His recent books include *Clinical Handbook of Psychological Disorders: A Step-by-Step Treatment Manual—Second Edition* (1993), *Anxiety and Its Disorders: The Nature and Treatment of Anxiety and Panic* (1988), and *Mastery of Your Anxiety and Panic—Second Edition and Agoraphobia Supplement Therapist Guide*, coauthored by Michelle Craske (1994).

Formerly, Dr. Barlow was professor of psychiatry and psychology at Brown University. He was also Distinguished Professor in the Department of Psychology, co-director of the Center for Stress and Anxiety Disorders, and director of the Phobia and Anxiety Disorders Clinic at the University at Albany—State University of New York. Currently, he is professor of psychology, director of the Clinical Training Program, and director of the Center for Anxiety and Related Disorders at Boston University. Dr. Barlow is also past president of the Division of Clinical Psychology of the American Psychological Association. He has been a consultant to the National Institute of Mental Health (NIMH) and the National Institutes of Health since 1973 and was recently awarded a merit award from the NIMH for "research competence and productivity that are distinctly superior." He was a member of the DSM–IV Task Force. The major objective of his work for the last 15 years has been the development of new treatments for anxiety disorders.

Acknowledgments

We are very grateful for all of the work that Michelle Barchi provided in helping us put together this book. She was always uncomplaining and cheerful through the many drafts, which required her to enter and reenter the text of the book. We are also thankful to Chris Gordon, who reviewed early drafts and helped shape the final version through his insightful comments. Finally, we would like to extend our thanks and acknowledge our indebtedness to John Wincze's administrative assistant, Sue Paquette, whose humor and support have helped him throughout the many years that they have worked together.

Sincere thanks are in order to The Psychological Corporation, especially to Aurelio Prifitera, PhD, and Sandra Prince–Embury, PhD, for their support in bringing this product to publication. As Project Director, Dr. Prince-Embury has contributed steady support and invaluable guidance to ensure scientific precision and clinical usability of the Client Workbook. John R. Dilworth, President of The Psychological Corporation, and Joanne Lenke, PhD, Executive Vice President, provided important administrative support. For much effort during the final stages of production of the *Enhancing Sexuality Client Workbook*, hearty thanks go to RaeLynn Alvarez and John Trent, Research Analysts; Terri C. Traeger, Supervising Editor; Cynthia Woerner, Consulting Editor; and Javier Flores, Designer. The contributions of Jo Boulet, Production Manager, are also much appreciated.

December, 1996

Chapter 1

Introduction

About This Workbook

The title of this Workbook is *Enhancing Sexuality: A Problem-Solving Approach*. From it, you will learn to improve and enjoy your sexual relations. At some point in life, almost all men and women have a problem with sexual functioning. The problem can cause frustration, stress, or depression. Many people take problems with sex in stride. For them, the problems are just short, unpleasant experiences. For many others, sex problems lead to the ruin of relationships. They also cause other problems. They can hurt a person's self-esteem. They can make a person anxious and depressed. They can lead to other problems with sex. If you are looking for solutions to sexual problems, this Workbook can help. It can help you solve those problems and prevent future ones. We recommend it as one part of professional treatment. First, you must commit yourself to doing what the Workbook suggests for your problem. In this way, you can learn ways to make your sex life enjoyable and satisfactory.

This Workbook gives correct information about sex. It reveals common myths and misunderstandings about sex. It gives information to help men and women to pinpoint the sources of problems and to find ways for solving them. It also shows ways to avoid certain "stumbling blocks" to progress.

Do You Have a Sexual Problem?

Both single people and couples seek help for sexual problems. These problems range from simple to complex. It is important to know that *any* problem can cause worry or depression. Some problems may be solved quickly with accurate information. For other problems, a person may need medical and psychological help. Your sex life might worry, depress, upset, or not fulfill you or your partner. If so, you may have a sexual problem. What you do sexually may not match what you think other people do. This does not mean you have problem. If you and your partner are happy with your sexual activity, you do not have a problem. For example, one couple may be perfectly happy having sex once a year. Another couple may be content only if they have sex five times a week. Neither way is a problem unless someone becomes unhappy with it.

Common Types of Sexual Problems

Most of the time, unhappiness with sex centers on two things. One is the frequency of sex. The other is the types of behaviors that are or are *not* part of a couple's sexual life. People enter therapy to change many things, in themselves or in their partners. They might want to change the level of desire for sex. They might want to agree on the type and variety of behaviors included in sex. They might want to improve specific sexual functions. These can be getting an erection, having an orgasm, or ejaculating.

The most common reason men enter therapy is a problem with erections. An erection or lack of an erection is something visible. So, a man and his partner usually know if there is a problem. Sometimes, partners might not agree because of partial erections. With a partial erection, the penis is not as firm, but intercourse can still occur. Because erection problems can be seen, there is more attention and pressure to "correct" them.

Another common problem is very quick ejaculation. Quick ejaculation happens most often to men aged 30 and younger. The problem is usually brought to therapy for two reasons. One reason is that it keeps happening. The other reason is that it hinders satisfaction with sex. In extreme cases, men may ejaculate as soon as their partners touch them. Most men who seek help for this problem ejaculate in less than 1 minute after intercourse starts. Other men think they have quick ejaculation problems when they really do not. What they believe about "how long they should last" is unrealistic. One young couple came for help because the woman thought that her fiancé should be able to last at least an hour! She was surprised to learn that most men ejaculate after 2–8 minutes.

Men who have a problem in having an orgasm in spite of firm erections also seek therapy. This problem is not as common as problems with erections or quick ejaculations. However, it is very upsetting to the men who have it.

Some men enter therapy because either they or their partners seem to lack sexual desire. It is important to find out if the problem is truly a lack of desire. A person might truly have no desire or might be avoiding sex in general. There must be two conditions for the problem to be a *true* lack of desire. One, a person does not pursue sex even if there is a willing, able, and attractive partner. Two, there is no other sexual problem.

A common problem for women who seek help is a feeling of emotional discomfort with sex. In some cases, the feelings connected with sex may be strong fear and anxiety. In other cases, it may be mild uneasiness. Discomfort with sex may occur as the only problem. It may occur along with some other sexual problem, such as a problem in having an orgasm. It is sometimes hard to separate emotional discomfort with sex from a lack of desire for sex. A lack of desire almost always goes with a discomfort with sex. The opposite is not always true. A discomfort with sex does not always mean a lack of desire. A woman may not actively want to have sex, but she may not have any discomfort with sex started by her partner. She may even enjoy it. However, when emotional discomfort with sex is the problem, the woman will not enjoy sex. The experience will be unpleasant and desire will be lacking. This is true even when the other conditions for sex are favorable. This combination of circumstances is much more common in women than in men.

Women may also seek therapy when their discomfort with sex has physical causes. In extreme cases, the vagina cannot be penetrated. The reason is vaginal muscle spasms. In other cases, penetration can occur but causes physical pain.

Some women who seek help may not have emotional or physical discomfort with sex. Instead, they may have a problem in reaching an orgasm.

Differences Between Men and Women

In most cultures, the sexual expectations for men and women differ. So, attitudes about sex will also differ. Men tend to focus on the *mechanics* of sex. Women tend to focus subjectively on the *meaning* of sex. Men are more likely to have sex because they have the opportunity and because others expect them to. Women are more likely to have sex because of their feelings. Of course, these gender differences are not always true. However, they do cause problems in sex relations between men and women.

Differences Between Partners

Case 1

After 6 years of marriage, Mr. and Mrs. W. came for help because they believed that Mrs. W. was not interested in sex. Mr. W. firmly believed that in marriage, sex should occur every other day. If a day for sex was missed, then Mr. W. believed they should make up for it by having sex 2 days in a row. Mrs. W. was guided more by feelings than by a formula. So, she participated in sex "only" four or five times a month. When she chose to participate in sex, she enjoyed it. Mr. W. could not understand why his wife did not want to have sex as often as he did. She seemed to

enjoy sex when she did participate. He labeled her behavior as "the problem." At the beginning of therapy, she accepted this label, too.

These different ideas about sex often make men and women also differ in their feelings about sex problems. Men often feel totally destroyed. Sometimes they even think about suicide when they have sexual problems. Many men frequently say they no longer feel like "real" men. They link their self-esteem to their sexual functioning. Women react differently to sex problems. They rarely have ideas of suicide or doubts about not being a "real" woman. Rather, women may become teary and sad or anxious about not being able to please their partners.

When his partner has a sex problem, a man often will say he feels "gypped" and angry over his not being fulfilled. A woman, on the other hand, is more likely to say she feels unloved and rejected. Women may express anger because they feel rejected. Men express anger because of feeling that they are not getting what they deserve or believe they were promised.

What Causes Sexual Problems?

Many factors can affect satisfaction with sex. Men and women must understand this to understand the causes of a sex problem. The factor can have to do with biology, psychology, or the situation. Sexual problems are often caused by more than one factor. So, pinning all of the blame on one factor is often wrong, misleading, and *unhelpful*. Biological factors that may lead to sex problems can do so through direct or indirect paths. A *direct* path directly affects being able to have sex. A direct path can be a disease, surgery, injury, or medicine. For example, diabetes affects nerve impulses and blood flow. These are important to sexual functioning in both men and women. An *indirect* path is any physical factor that affects how a person feels. How a person feels affects how he or she functions sexually. However, it does not itself directly cause the sex problem. For example, a cold may make a person feel lousy and therefore not in the mood for sex. However, a cold does not physically keep a person from being able to have sex.

Psychological factors have to do with a person's learning history. These factors include a person's sexual knowledge. They also include a person's emotions, fears, attitudes, and skills with regard to sex.

Situation factors are factors *outside* of the person. These include time, place, and partner issues. For example, a couple may have very different work schedules. So, they may have little quality time for each other. A person may have a partner with many medical problems. These problems can cause the partner to have little interest in sex.

Factors That Can Cause Problems

Case 2

Mr. and Mrs. C. had been married for 22 years. Mr. C. was a successful businessman. When he came for help for erection problems, his business was failing. He was also obese and had had diabetes for 10 years. Mrs. C. did not work outside her home. She was very involved in the activities of her two sons (aged 16 and 20). For example, she made breakfast for her younger son every day even though he could make his own breakfast. She also drove him to hockey practice at 5:30 a.m., even though he had his driver's license.

Mrs. C. had a very strict religious upbringing in which sex was never discussed. When she married, she had no sexual experience. She stated that she never enjoyed sex during the marriage.

Mr. C.'s erection problem is an example of a problem that may have many causes. Diabetes is a direct physical factor. Being obese is an indirect factor. It can affect self-esteem and desire. Mr. C.'s worry about his failing business may be a psychological factor. It could have prevented him from enjoying sex. There are also some situation factors that could affect Mr. C.'s erection problem. These are Mrs. C.'s dislike for sex, lack of experience, and being so involved with her children (and not with her husband).

There is another fact about sex problems that men and women need to understand. The current cause of a sex problem might not be the original cause. For example, a man might have first had erection failure because he tried to have sex when he was drunk. The erection failure might have embarrassed him. Then, he worried that it would happen again, even when he was not drinking. The current problem could be caused by worry over past problems, even though the original cause was a night of drinking.

Do You Fit This Workbook?

Most problems and help in this Workbook have little to do with a person's sexual preference. This Workbook is for people who are attracted to persons of the opposite gender or the same gender. It is also for people who are attracted to persons of either gender. So far, we have talked about how common sex problems are and types of common problems. We have also talked about how men and women differ in their sex problems and causes of sex problems. With this information, you can begin to ask yourself some questions. "Does this sound like me (or us)?" "Can my (our) problem be helped by this Workbook?"

There are other questions to think about: Are you avoiding sexual relations? Are you upset or unhappy with your sexual relations? Are you angry with your partner because of sex problems? Is your partner angry with you because of sex problems? Do you think that you are unattractive? Do you feel inexperienced about sex? Do you feel unskilled or insecure about sex?

If you answered "yes" to any of these questions, then this Workbook could be helpful. It may not be helpful if you are currently abusing alcohol or other drugs. Abuse of alcohol or other drugs must be treated before sex problems can be treated with success.

What Benefits Will You Receive From This Workbook?

This Workbook can help you whether or not you are currently with a steady partner. What should you expect to gain from this Workbook? Research shows that therapy is very effective in treating sex problems (see Suggested Readings for more information). Each person's case is unique, and there is no guarantee that your problem will be completely "cured." However, this Workbook should help those who are *motivated*. At the very least, you will gain an understanding of the factors that cause sex problems. You will learn ways to increase sexual satisfaction. You will also learn how to set realistic goals for yourself and how to obtain more pleasure from your sex life.

You might have a partner who is not interested or who is against working with you to solve your sex problem. If so, then this Workbook may not be as helpful. The same is true if you are having very destructive marriage problems and are thinking about divorce. If you are in therapy for marriage problems, however, this Workbook can be a part of that treatment.

Using This Workbook With a Therapist

This Workbook is designed to be used with the help of a professional therapist. You and your therapist will decide the specific frequency or type of treatment. Therapy is helpful for issues that are too emotional or hard for you to handle alone. Many couples can deal with issues only in therapy. At home, they avoid or become too upset with certain topics. For example, a sexual problem may be linked to one partner's being unfaithful. Talking about such a problem alone at home can quickly turn into an outburst of emotions. This kind of discussion does not help. A therapist can help you use the emotions in a productive way and help solve the problems.

Often, couples who have been together for a while seem to have many issues they wish to discuss. When they talk about one problem, however, others often show up. A couple may end up not solving anything when too many issues are brought up at once. A therapist can help a couple to stay on track and to resolve one issue before going on to another. Also, most couples and individuals have a hard time dealing with sex problems on their own. The reason is that sex is not a topic that is openly and comfortably discussed. Strong emotions and poor communication can make things even harder. For all these reasons, a therapist is very helpful to people who are dealing with sex problems.

Brief Description of the Workbook

The Workbook is divided into 12 chapters or lessons. Each chapter presents specific skills that build on each other. So, each new chapter asks you to use the skills you learned before. Even though the Workbook is designed this way, you can tailor it to fit your needs. Chapters about problems that you are not having may be skipped.

At the end of each chapter is a review. It can help you decide whether or not you have learned the important information from that chapter. If you think you have not learned the information, you should go over the chapter again. This point is very important because each step is based on what you learned in previous steps. If you believe you have understood the material, then go on to the next chapter. Also, each chapter has specific exercises at the end. We designed these exercises after years of work with hundreds of people. Your progress and success with the Workbook depend on doing the exercises. Worksheets are provided with some of the chapters for you or you and a partner to complete.

This Workbook is also divided into three sections. Chapters 1–4 give basic information. They discuss how men and women develop sex behavior. They also discuss the types of common sex problems and the ways men and women react to them. These chapters give you the information you will need to understand and assess your specific problem.

Chapters 5–7 describe the nature of specific sex problems that men and women have. The purpose is to help you completely understand the most common causes of your problem. Often the problem stems from a combination of factors. When you understand the factors, you will be ready for the final section of the Workbook. The final section can help you overcome your problem with specific ways of treating it.

Chapters 8–12 focus on treatment and prevention for specific sex problems. Most of the information in this section applies to all sex problems.

Chapter 2

Learning About Your Reactions to Sexual Problems

With this chapter, you will begin to learn that false ideas and false information about sex are common. These false ideas can make a person feel inadequate. They can also cause problems between sexual partners. People can believe false ideas for years. One major reason is that most people are too afraid or too embarrassed to ask questions about sex. This chapter and the exercise at the end will alert you to some common misbeliefs about sex. They will also help you to begin discussing sexual matters.

You can use Worksheet 2.1 to list myths about sex that you once believed but now know are incorrect. You can also list beliefs that you are not sure about. Compare these lists to what you learn from this chapter and from the exercise at the end.

Men's Reactions to Their Own Sexual Problems

Most cultures have double standards about what they expect for men and women with regard to sex. The message to men often is that they should be sexual at every chance. The message to women is to hold back their sexuality. From Chapter 1, you know that these differences can cause men and women to react to sex problems in very different ways. Men are expected to always be sexual. Perhaps this is the reason they feel so devastated when they are not able to be sexual. When they feel ashamed and devastated, most men avoid sex or isolate themselves. Some men react this way immediately. This is true especially in cases of erection failure. A man who has a partner may avoid sex. He does this by going to bed at a different time than his partner or by not showing affection. Often, men think, "I don't want to start something I can't finish."

A single man may avoid dating. He may think, "I don't want to put myself in a situation that might embarrass or shame me." He may think, "I don't want to date until I can guarantee that I will function *perfectly*." Sadly, avoiding sex almost always brings on more problems.

Some men who are having sex problems try to "test out" having sex in other situations or with other partners. A man might test out in different ways. He might masturbate or use sexy magazines. He might try to have sex with a prostitute or a new partner. Many men find, however, that they have the problem in these other situations, too. Even if the problem is all psychological, the "pressure to perform" is still great. That pressure ruins anything in the new situation that might have helped. Chapter 5 talks about the positive and negative factors for sex.

In summary, many men who have sex problems avoid facing their problem. Some start avoiding sex right away. Others start avoiding sex after they have tried testing out. Most men think that testing out in other situations is less threatening. Sadly, men often take the pressure to perform with them into these circumstances. So, they fail again. That failure makes them feel even more inadequate.

We are not advising you to test out your sexual functioning. The decision to test out or how you might test out is a personal one. We are saying that when men test out, they often do so under the same pressure to perform that they feel with their partners. Remember, sex "works" best when you focus on pleasure rather than on performance. Also, some men who have sex problems with their main partners do not place any value on other sexual successes. They do so because they believe the myth that men should *always* be ready for sex and *always* be able to respond. Therefore, these successes do not "count."

Men's Reactions to Their Partners' Sexual Problems

When the man's partner is the one with a sex problem, the man may react in a number of ways. How a man reacts depends on the problem. Some men may hardly notice the problem. Others may become angry. Some men may not notice the problem because they do not expect women to enjoy sex. Sex will go on without complaint as long as the man is able to complete intercourse. Some men have bragged to us that their partners are "always available for sex" or "have never turned them down." Such a relationship may not be very satisfying for the woman. It is not likely that any woman is "in the mood" every time her partner wants sex. The man probably does not notice that the woman has little desire, does not have an orgasm, and receives very little pleasure.

Sometimes sex becomes less frequent or stops because of a partner's sex problem. In these cases, the man often responds with anger or mistrust. A man will respond this way especially if he views sex as part of the "duties" of his partner. In some cases, the anger may result in abuse or threats of "getting it elsewhere."

Women's Reactions to Their Own Sexual Problems

Women are more likely than men to view minor sex problems as inconveniences. Sometimes a woman's sex problem is more extreme and causes pain or psychological stress. The woman then usually avoids sex. Even in these cases, however, a woman rarely thinks of herself as less of a woman.

Women with sex problems often will not start or respond to affection. They (and men) believe that once a man is aroused, he must "go all the way." A male partner may even become angry and say, "Don't start something unless you can finish it." Such beliefs and attitudes only keep a problem going and do not help solve the problem. The same is not true in lesbian partnerships. When one partner has a sex problem, avoiding all physical contact may be less common. Most of the time, women in lesbian partnerships do not hold an all-or-none view of sex.

Women's Reactions to Their Partners' Sexual Problems

At first, a woman often reacts to her partner's sex problem with hurt, anger, and mistrust. A woman might think, "My partner is having a sex problem because he or she is involved with or attracted to someone else." She might think, "My partner is having a sex problem because he or she no longer finds me attractive." These thoughts can occur in a partnership with a man. They can also occur in a lesbian partnership. With either thought, hurt and anger are much more likely.

Insecurities and Misunderstanding Can Cause Problems

Case 3

Mr. and Mrs. E. entered therapy because Mr. E. was having erection problems. The couple had been married for 7 years. Mr. E. was 53, and Mrs. E. was 35. Mrs. E. was extremely upset by Mr. E.'s sexual problem. She accused him of not finding her attractive. She also stated that normal men are always ready for sex and are always able to function. She said this with very strong conviction.

Mr. E. stated that he was very much attracted to his wife. He also said that he was not interested in or involved with another woman. He described his wife as very, very insecure and in need of a lot of reassurance. She was this way despite being attractive. Mrs. E. was always putting pressure on him for sex. She would belittle him when he was "not in the mood."

Mrs. E. also believed that once a man was married, he should be not attracted to other women. Also, once married, a man should not

masturbate. Mrs. E. would watch Mr. E. carefully when other women were around to see if he seemed to be attracted to them.

Mrs. E. was insecure and had misunderstandings about sex. These two things helped to cause and keep up the sex problems of this couple. Mrs. E.'s beliefs about sex are not unusual. Therapists have come across similar beliefs many times. Mrs. E. learned her beliefs from her previous short-term relationships. Most of the time, the focus of short-term relationships is on sexual pleasure. This focus may cover up many factors that can interfere with sex. In a long-term partnership, a couple must put more effort into making sure that sex brings pleasure.

Movies, books, and magazines also keep up the belief that a man can function no matter what. All he needs is a willing partner (or even a partner playing "hard to get," as in *Gone With the Wind*). The leading men in many movies have shown this. They perform sexually, even after going through things that would ruin most other men. Therefore, Mrs. E. likely had a lot of support for her beliefs. Her knowledge and past relationships did not prepare her for the changes in sex that occur in a long partnership.

Mrs. E. thought Mr. E. should not to be attracted to other women after marriage. This belief is not reasonable. Being attracted to others is natural. It is a part of our physical makeup. It continues for most people throughout their lives, married or not. In marriage, one should not act on an outside attraction. However, the attraction itself is normal and understandable in both men and women.

Exercise: What Are Your Sexual Beliefs?

Sex in general and sex problems in particular are hard for most people to discuss. Couples may live with sexual problems for years. They react with avoidance and anger and hurt, yet they never directly discuss their problems. Many of these feelings and reactions come from false ideas and false beliefs about sex. Read Appendix A, "Common Sexual Myths." It will help you to be more at ease in talking about sexual matters. It will also help you learn about your beliefs. After you and your partner read Appendix A, discuss it with each other. It is important that you set aside a specific time for the talk. This time should be when you will not be interrupted or distracted in any way. Unplug telephones, turn off the television, and put the children to bed. Doing these things will create a good environment for talking. Your discussion should focus on what *myths* each of you believes and how you got and kept these beliefs. One purpose of this exercise is to make discussions about sex easier. Another purpose is to help you to learn about your own beliefs and those of your partner. *This is not an exercise to prove who is right or wrong.* It is a fact-finding exercise. Try to avoid arguments. How does your list of sexual myths compare to the list in Appendix A?

Chapter 2 Review

Answer by circling **T** (True) or **F** (False). Answers are provided in Appendix B.

1. Masturbation by a man or a woman is a sign that
    something is wrong with his or her sex life.   **T**   **F**

2. A man should always be able to get an erection if
    he is with an attractive and willing partner.   **T**   **F**

3. One of the most common reactions to a sex problem
    for men and women is to avoid sex.   **T**   **F**

4. It is common for women who are having sex problems
    to "test out" to see if sex will "work" in other situations.   **T**   **F**

5. If a man or woman is not able to have sex, it is best for
    the couple to avoid all physical affection.   **T**   **F**

Worksheet 2.1. Sexual Myths

Sexual myths I now know are not factual:

1. _____
2. _____
3. _____
4. _____
5. _____

Sexual myths that I'm not sure about:

1. _____
2. _____
3. _____
4. _____
5. _____

Worksheet 2.1. Sexual Myths

Sexual myths I now know are not factual:

1. _____

2. _____

3. _____

4. _____

5. _____

Sexual myths that I'm not sure about:

1. _____

2. _____

3. _____

4. _____

5. _____

Chapter 3

Understanding Your Sexuality

Here, we talk about the things in a person's life that affect the way he or she develops sexually. It is important for you to understand why you are sexually the way you are. Use Worksheet 3.1 to write down important things in your life that might have affected your sexual development. By "sexual development," we mean a lot of things. It includes how you feel about your body and how comfortable you feel about sex. It also has to do with what types of people sexually attract you. Finally, it means how you act sexually.

If you answered "No" to any of the questions listed on Worksheet 3.1, write down why you answered "No." Your answers will help you begin to know why you have developed sexually the way you have. Your answers will also be used as part of the exercise at the end of this chapter.

How Sexuality Patterns Develop

Think about the things that interest you sexually. Think about the way you behave sexually. Did you ever wonder why you are different from other people you know? Why is it that you are attracted to a one type of person, but others are not? Why are some people perfectly at ease with hugging and other signs of affection? Why do other people not like to be touched at all? Why do some people like to be treated roughly during sex and others like a slow, gentle approach? The ways that you act sexually and the people who attract you make up parts of your sexual pattern. In this chapter, we focus on how and why this pattern develops. By knowing this, you will understand better why you and your partner (if you have one) behave the way you do. In this way, you can accept, not judge, the ways other people sexually differ from you.

Some of the things that affect your sexual behavior and interests may be genetic. For example, genes might decide how responsive you are physically. Others might affect how coordinated you are and the size and shape of your body. Other genes decide the way you look. In this way, these factors may at least partly affect your sexual skills and appearance. These genetic factors are *not* within your control. What you learn about sex during your life is what mostly decides your sexual behavior and interests. You learn from what you have observed or heard in the course of growing up. You also learn from what you have directly experienced. Both of these strongly determine your sexual pattern. So, most aspects of your sexual behavior or sexual likes come from what you have learned.

Childhood Experiences

Most children, by age 2 or 3, identify themselves as boys or girls. This is called *gender identity*. Your gender identity is different from gender roles that you may play. *Gender roles* are behaviors or activities that are typical of a gender. So, men more often than women will be construction workers. Women more often than men will be secretaries. It is perfectly normal for a woman to be a construction worker. It is perfectly normal for a man to be a secretary. These roles are just not typical. Your gender role is separate from gender identity. In most cultures, gender roles are becoming more and more flexible.

What you experience as a child has a big impact on both gender identity and gender role. From the time you were born, your parents and other adults in your life referred to you as a boy or a girl. They treated you in certain ways "appropriate" for your gender. An infant boy is often treated as "tough" and "strong." An infant girl may be treated as "pretty" and "delicate." Experts believe that such messages help shape our gender identities as boys or girls. Many things help shape your gender role. One thing is the roles that you see the adults around you play. Another thing is the toys you are encouraged to play with. Yet another thing is the messages you receive about your future roles in society.

As a child, you also learn your *sexual direction*. This is a person's attraction to people of the same gender or to those of the opposite gender. Everyone differs in how strongly he or she is attracted to a gender. Some people are attracted to both men and women. When a person is attracted to both men and women, it is called *bisexuality*. Having an attraction does not mean that the person will *act* on his or her attraction. People may act on their attraction only with men or only with women, even though they are attracted to both. The experiences that you have as a child shape sexual direction. Experts are still not sure which experiences are the ones that shape sexual directions.

As a child, you also learn your *sexual behavior*. This means how you express yourself in sexual activity. What you learned as a child can affect your frequency of sex behavior and your approach to sex. It also affects how you act during sexual encounters. One of the most important sexual behaviors is your comfort level with sex. Many things affect your comfort level with sex. Some of these things are your attitude toward sex, what you know about sex, and what you experienced as you grew up. For example, some parents give their children "warnings" about sex. At the same time, they do not give them the idea that sex can also be good and enjoyable. This could make you grow up not feeling very at ease with sex unless you also had good messages from a source other than your parents. Most parents have difficulty talking to their children about sex. So, people grow up learning about sex from many sources. They learn from friends, television and movies, and their parents' behavior.

Perhaps you never saw your parents show affection toward each other. Perhaps you never felt affection as a child. If so, you might not be comfortable with affection, such as touching or hugging, as an adult. Bad experiences can also affect your sex life. These are sexual abuse and sexual contact that is not wanted. They affect your attitudes toward sex and the way you behave sexually.

Unwanted Sex and Its Consequences

Case 4

> Mr. and Mrs. H. had been married 10 years when they came to therapy for help with a sex problem. Both were very attractive and well educated. They showed much love toward each other. The problem was that Mrs. H. was very uneasy with any foreplay, even though she was comfortable with intercourse. She did not like to touch her husband and did not like for him to touch her. She had been able to enjoy touching and foreplay during the first few years of their marriage. Then, something changed. Now, Mr. and Mrs. H. were in their early thirties. Their sex life was becoming a source of argument and unhappiness.
>
> A review of their backgrounds showed that they both came from warm and loving families. Sadly, Mrs. H. had an older male cousin who had put pressure on her and tricked her into sex activities. This unwanted sex occurred over and over during many years. It included fondling and masturbating. It did *not* include intercourse. This repeated, unwanted sex very likely had a negative effect on Mrs. H. It likely led to Mrs. H.'s discomfort with foreplay in her marriage. At the beginning of the marriage, love and excitement must have overcome the bad feelings from the past. In time, as sex between husband and wife became more routine, the old emotional pain took over.

What Mrs. H. went through as a child should not be confused with the normal sex play that most children go through. It is usual for children of about the same age to play in many ways that seem sexual. Actually, boys and girls, boys and boys, and girls and girls (everybody) often touch, look, hug, and kiss. Such behavior (*especially* in children under age 6) is not at all harmful and should not be punished. Mrs. H.'s experience as a child was very different and harmful. Her cousin was able to trick her over and over into doing things that made her very uneasy. Unlike play that is normal for a child, what Mrs. H went through was not wanted and was not voluntary.

Teenage Sexual Experiences

Teenage years are hard for many people. It is the time of our lives when we learn about ourselves and begin to be more independent from our parents. The most important stage during teenage years (or late childhood) is *puberty*. During this time, boys and girls grow hair on their genitals and under their arms. Girls develop breasts and begin to menstruate (have their periods). Boys have frequent erections and nocturnal emissions ("wet dreams"), and their voices deepen. These changes can be very positive. Both boys and girls begin to feel their sexuality. Also, boys and girls begin to have attraction to others and to notice that other teenagers are attracted to them.

For some people, puberty can be a disaster. Some parents do not understand about the sexual changes that teens go through. Growing up with such parents can be very upsetting. One woman told us that when she was 11 years old, her mother forcibly held her while her father put a training bra on her. Her parents had never explained anything to her about puberty. They thought she was being disrespectful to them by not wanting to wear a bra. One man told us that his mother would burst into the bathroom to see if he was masturbating.

Puberty may also be hard because of other teenagers. They can often be cruel. The changes in our bodies may bring unwanted staring and teasing from others. As a result, teens often feel insecure and uneasy. Teens also often have low self-esteem. All of these things can keep teens from wanting to do anything social or sexual.

For many of us, our first experiences with sex occur during our teen years. What you are taught by your family, culture, and religion guide you to act or not to act on your sexual urges. The chance to act sexually is also a factor. Your self-esteem and comfort with your body are also factors. All these things affect whether or not you make opportunities for sex happen and whether you act or do not act on them.

During the teen years, a person can be very unsure and very vulnerable. Perhaps you thought you were too fat or too skinny. Perhaps you thought you were too tall or too short. Perhaps you had acne. These things can affect a person very deeply. They can cause the person to be very insecure and to have low self-esteem. Such a person is likely to avoid social contact and to isolate himself or herself. This may keep a person from exploring anything sexual. It also helps to maintain low self-esteem. When such a person acts on an opportunity for sex, he or she often brings along a focus on how he or she performs. The main concern is doing things right to avoid rejection or failure. This focus is often the first step toward sex problems.

Masturbation and Sexual Fantasies

People often start to masturbate and to have sex fantasies as a child or young teenager. Most of the time, masturbating is normal. For some people, it becomes excessive. It begins to interfere with a person's life. For most people, it is a way of getting rid of sexual energy or frustration. This causes no problems whatsoever. It may go on throughout life even if a person is in a loving, adult relationship.

Most people use sex fantasies when they masturbate. These fantasies are often the most arousing images a person can think of. They are only fantasies. They are not necessarily something a person would really do. It is quite common for a fantasy to go beyond what most people think is legal or moral. It is not the *fantasizing about* something that is a problem. It is the *acting on* something unacceptable that is the problem.

Sex fantasies are important for teens. They are a safe way to practice sexual activities. At times, however, a teenager may be upset by his or her sexual daydreams. This happens when the thoughts seem weird to them. Most teenagers do not have much experience with or knowledge about sex. So, they might think unusual sexual daydreams are not normal. For example, a young boy has no idea if his daydreams about his sitter are "okay." People rarely talk about these daydreams openly, even with a best friend. So, a person may become anxious about his or her fantasies. Very few people talk about these topics. So, it can take a long time for a young person to realize that many people share the same sexual thoughts.

By the end of the teen years, most people have had a sexual experience with someone. It is not normal and it is not abnormal to have had sex or not to have had sex. It is clear, though, that by the time a person becomes an adult, his or her sexual pattern is mostly set. Your comfort level with sex and the types of sexual behaviors you like or do not like are in place. The people who attract you and your self-confidence with regard to sex are also set. All of this is what you bring to your adult sex life.

Adult Sexual Experiences

Most people do not talk about sex. So, when they become adults, they bring along the fears and misunderstandings about sex that developed in the teen years. In an adult partnership, these fears and misunderstandings may cause problems. In a teen relationship, the teenager may simply move on to a new partner when problems come up. In this way, the teenager avoids any need to solve problems.

For a committed partnership to stay healthy, the couple must work out conflicts and problems they have with sex. Sadly, many people do not have the things they need to do this. They do not have the comfort level or the know-how to identify, discuss, and solve sex problems. Problems may emerge only after a few years of marriage. This was the case with Mr. and Mrs. H.

Fear of Sex

Case 5

Mr. and Mrs. J. came to therapy because of Mrs. J.'s extreme fear of sex. She feared sex so much that she could not even say the words *vagina* and *penis*. Unlike Mrs. H. in the previous case, Mrs. J. had no history of sexual abuse. Her fears developed from something else. She was raised by two very overprotective parents. Both parents feared many aspects of life and were very moralistic. They openly condemned anything that had to do with sex. Then, Mrs. J.'s older, unmarried sister became pregnant. The family reacted as though the sister had died. Mrs. J. became the "good" sister. Without knowing it, she denied her own sexual being. She could not look at her own body in the mirror. She could not enjoy touching or being touched. She thought of such activities as "bad."

In spite of all of this, Mrs. J. was able to enjoy sex for many months after marriage. Soon, however, she began to withdraw and to avoid sex. Mr. J. felt rejected and angry. Therapy was the only thing that helped Mrs. J. pinpoint the source of her discomfort with sex. Then, her problem was put into perspective and treated. When many people marry, they expect any sex problems they had just to go away. This does not happen. Instead, the problem leads the person to withdraw and to avoid sex within the marriage. It can also lead to the end of the marriage or relationship.

Sometimes a problem comes up in an adult partnership for other reasons. One reason is that a couple expect and believe different things about sex. Each partner must understand that the other has sex expectations and patterns that differ from his or her own. Partners must also understand something else. Such differences are common and normal. In most cases, the differences will be minor. Also, the couple can make adjustments through trial and error. When major differences do exist, the couple must do something else. They have to see the differences as *differences*, *not* as right or wrong. When behavior is seen as right or wrong, partners blame each other, and arguments can occur.

Most of the time, when people become adults they improve the sex skills that came from the sex patterns they learned when they were children and teens. Rarely as adults can people completely change their sex patterns. They can learn new behaviors within the patterns. Most of the time, they will not develop totally new sexual interests.

The following list defines the key terms used in this chapter. Table 3.1 summarizes those things that can affect a person's sexuality.

Key Terms in Sexual Development

- *Gender identity*—The belief we have about whether we are male or female
- *Gender role*—The attitudes and behaviors we have that are thought to be normal, appropriate, and common for a gender (male or female)
- *Sexual behavior*—How we act in a sexual way
- *Sexual pattern*—The way we respond with feelings of sexual arousal or interest, including the types of people who attract us and the behaviors we enjoy

Table 3.1. **Summary of Important Influences on the Development of Sexuality**

Stage of Life	Normal Sexual Development	Potential Positive Influences During This Stage	Potential Negative Influences During This Stage
Infancy and Childhood *(Ages 0–12)*	Gender identity as male or female Exploration of one's own genitals and body Exploration of body with an equal-age peer (up to 6 years of age) Beginning of sexual feelings Beginning of self pleasure—masturbation Beginning of sexual fantasies	Parents who give(s) sex information and guidance Verbal and physical affection from parents Positive and reaffirming messages from parents about your sexuality and your body	Sexual experience with older person, with or without coercion Lack of verbal or physical affection from parents Negative messages about sex in absence of positive messages or guidance

Stage of Life	Normal Sexual Development	Potential Positive Influences During This Stage	Potential Negative Influences During This Stage
Adolescence or Teenage Years *(Ages 13–19)*	Changes in our bodies (puberty) Firmly established sexual patterns Initial consensual sexual experiences (may or may not include intercourse) Continued masturbation Continued sexual fantasies	Parents who give sex information and guidance (especially regarding puberty and sexual feelings and activity) Verbal and physical affection from parents Positive and reaffirming messages from parents about your sexuality and your body	Coercive or upsetting sexual experiences Degrading or teasing comments about one's bodily changes Lack of sexual guidance or support from parent Isolation from peers
Adult Years *(Ages 20+)*	Involvement in consensual sexual activity Exploring variations of sexual activity within one's sexual pattern Continued masturbation Continued sexual fantasies	A supportive sexual partner who is easy to communicate with Accurate sexual information and guidance to address any sexual concerns or anxieties	An unsupportive critical partner with inflexible, rigid ideas about what is "right" and "wrong" in sex Coercive or upsetting sexual experiences

Exercise

This exercise will help you better understand the things that have made you a sexual person. In Chapter 2, you started to learn how to communicate about sex. This exercise will also help you continue to improve in this area. We suggest that you follow the same rules that were in Chapter 2 to make sure you have private quality time with your partner. Again, set a time when you and your partner are relaxed and cannot be interrupted. For this exercise, focus on the past good and bad influences on your sexuality. Include good and bad things from your childhood and teen years. Also talk about issues that have to do with gender identity and gender roles. Include anything that could affect your sexual direction and patterns. This discussion may take more than one session.

Chapter 3 Review

Answer by circling **T** (True) or **F** (False). Answers are provided in Appendix B.

1. Genetic factors have the strongest effect on how a person grows sexually.　**T　F**

2. Sexual direction refers to what arouses you or turns you on.　**T　F**

3. It is normal to have sexual daydreams that include things that a person would not actually do.　**T　F**

4. It is not normal for a man or woman who is married to masturbate.　**T　F**

5. If you and your partner enjoyed sex together at one time but do not now, it means that you are no longer in love.　**T　F**

Worksheet 3.1. Influences on Your Sexual Development

1. Did your parents show affection toward each other? ☐ Yes ☐ No

2. Did your parents show affection toward you? ☐ Yes ☐ No

3. Did your parents give you positive messages about sex? ☐ Yes ☐ No

4. Did you always have a positive image of your body? ☐ Yes ☐ No

5. Were your first experiences with sex pleasant and of your choosing? ☐ Yes ☐ No

Worksheet 3.1. Influences on Your Sexual Development

1. Did your parents show affection toward each other? ☐ Yes ☐ No

2. Did your parents show affection toward you? ☐ Yes ☐ No

3. Did your parents give you positive messages about sex? ☐ Yes ☐ No

4. Did you always have a positive image of your body? ☐ Yes ☐ No

5. Were your first experiences with sex pleasant and of your choosing? ☐ Yes ☐ No

Chapter 4

Medical Factors That Affect Sexual Functioning

Diseases That Directly Affect Sexual Functioning

Some diseases have a *direct* effect on physically being able to have sex. These diseases affect the amount of blood flow or the speed of nerve impulses to the sex organs. Other diseases may not have a direct effect on the physical process of sex. They have an *indirect* effect by making a person feel less interested in sex.

Diabetes, heart disease, cancer, and multiple sclerosis are the diseases that most often have a direct effect on being able to have sex (see Suggested Readings for more information). These diseases hinder the flow of blood to the genitals or slow down nerve impulses. Most of the time, the effects of these diseases appear slowly over time. The effects can occur over a period of months or even a period of years. The first thing men usually notice is a less firm erection. The first thing women notice is trouble with vaginal wetness or with having an orgasm. The effects may not only happen slowly over time. The impact of these diseases is also somewhat uneven. At times, a person's ability to have sex may seem perfectly normal. At other times, it is less than satisfactory.

When things "don't work" during sex just one time, most men and women worry a lot. They focus on the next time they have sex. This *worry and negative focus* can cause even more problems with sex. Then, finding the exact cause of the problem can be even harder. Either physical disease or mental factors can affect the process of sex. The two together can cause a problem.

There is only one way a man will know that his erection problems are mostly due to disease factors. That way is when he does not have erections under *any* conditions. That is, he does not have erections when he sleeps, masturbates, or watches sexy movies. He also does not have erections with different partners or with his usual partner.

Some physical injuries can hinder being able to have sex. For example, spinal cord injury can do this. Surgical procedures can also affect being able to have sex. This happens when certain nerves are cut during the surgery. When injury or surgery is the cause, the loss of function happens right away and is total most of the time.

Physical Problems That Indirectly Affect Sexual Functioning

Physical problems sometimes "get in the way" and keep sex from being the best it can be. Many diseases and physical conditions might make you not want sex. This is so because of the way you feel or because of the disease's impact on your self-confidence. For example, even a common cold can take away your desire for sex because colds make you feel lousy. Also, a skin rash or being overweight can make you feel less attractive. If you feel less attractive, you are less likely to feel like being intimate with someone. Physical factors that make a person lose confidence can affect a person's sex life for a long time. Being overweight and severe acne in the teenage years are examples. They can set off a pattern of low self-esteem and social withdrawal. Such effects are often linked to a lack of sexual confidence. This may carry over to sexual relationships the person has as an adult.

Disease and physical factors can affect your desire for sex and your response to sex. These effects can be direct and indirect. It is important to understand this point. Then, you can explore these areas in trying to understand why you are the sexual person you are.

Prescription Medications That Affect Sexual Functioning

There is not a single drug that affects everyone the same way. This is one of the most important things to know about prescription drugs and sex. You cannot predict which drugs will interfere with your sex life and which ones will not. Certain types of drugs can have a negative effect on sex for many people who take them. Many people who take the same drug find out that their sex lives improve after taking the drug.

There has been little "controlled" research on the effects of drugs on sexual functioning. In a controlled research study, some of the people in the study take the real drug and some take a fake drug. (A fake drug is called a *placebo*.) The people do not know which one they are taking. Most information about these effects comes from what patients tell their doctors. This information has some value, but it cannot be relied on totally (see Suggested Readings for more information).

Also, most information about the effects of drugs on sex is about men. Fewer studies are about the effects on sex in women. In men, drugs can cause different problems. These are not being able to get an erection or losing desire for sex.

Others have to do with ejaculation. Drugs can cause some men to ejaculate too quickly or too slowly. For women, most drug studies focus on desire problems and on being able to have an orgasm (see Suggested Readings for more information).

Antidepressant Medication

Many kinds of prescribed drugs are often connected to sex problems. Depression is very common in adults. Most of the time, it is treated with antidepressant drugs. Reports show that these drugs have negative effects on the erections in men. They also decrease the desire for sex in both men and women. For men, the most common problems are ejaculating too slowly or not being able to ejaculate. In women, it is not being able to have an orgasm. This is called *anorgasmia*. All of the reports on these drugs also had good news. The side effects went away about 1 week after the drug was stopped. (see Suggested Readings for more information).

Antipsychotic Medication

Antipsychotic drugs are used to treat mental disorders. Two of these disorders are schizophrenia and paranoia. Both men and women who take these drugs have reported sex problems. The impact of these drugs is hard to determine exactly. However, research shows that people who take them likely had sex problems *before* taking the drugs. Even so, men who take them most often report problems with ejaculation. Women most often report problems with reaching an orgasm. Sex problems usually appear 1–2 weeks after the person starts taking the drug. Sex problems go away after the person stops taking the drug (see Suggested Readings for more information).

High Blood-Pressure Medication

There are many different drugs used to treat high blood pressure. These drugs work by slowing down or by regulating the heart. They also work by making blood vessels bigger or smaller. Reports state that these drugs most often affect men in two ways. They interfere with erections or they decrease the desire for sex. There have been very few controlled research studies on the effects of these drugs on sex. However, there is a widespread belief that they do cause sex problems for men. There are also very few reports about the effects of these drugs on sex in women (see Suggested Readings for more information).

Even when research on the sexual side effects of these drugs is well controlled, the results are not always clear. Erections in men do not stop automatically. In fact, for some men, erections improve with these drugs. Remember that there is a widespread belief that these drugs will have a negative effect. This belief is enough to worry men and cause them to have erection problems.

If you had sex problems only after you started taking the drug, then you should talk to your doctor. You and your doctor may find another drug that can control your high blood pressure and not cause sex problems. *Do not stop taking your medicine under any circumstances without first talking to your doctor.*

There are many other prescribed drugs that might have an effect on sexual functioning. The three types of drugs just discussed are the most common ones. There are reports of sexual side effects for "street" drugs also.

Street Drugs and Sexual Functioning

Most people think that street drugs make sexual functioning better. There is no proof for this belief. In fact, street drugs are more likely to interfere with sexual functioning. Most of the information is not based on reliable, controlled studies. Most of it is based on reports from drug users. Researchers compare reports that a certain drug makes sex better to reports that the same drug causes sex problems. Most of the time, the drug users do not tell how much of the drug they use or about other drugs they were using at the same time. Their reports also do not include their sexual histories. So, such information is just an "educated guess."

A lot has been written about the effects of marijuana, cocaine, and heroin on sex. Good and bad reports about sexual functioning exist for all classes of drugs (see Suggested Readings for more information).

On the good side, both men and women report that marijuana makes them have more pleasure and more intense orgasms. On the bad side, men and women mention having a lower sex drive and being less able to function. Most of the time, bad effects are connected to chronic use. Studies of the effects of marijuana on sex have focused on a certain male hormone. This hormone is testosterone. Marijuana first makes the testosterone level go up and then it makes go down. This hormone is very important for sex arousal in men. So, clearly, marijuana may have bad effects on sex response (Buffum, 1982).

Cocaine is another drug that has effects on sexual response. Its effects cannot be predicted. Some men report that it makes them have spontaneous erections. Some women report that it makes them have frequent multiple orgasms. There are also many reports of bad effects. These are not being able to get an erection, to ejaculate, or to have an orgasm. There is no reliable response among those who use cocaine. Also, there are no controlled studies of how this drug affects sexuality.

Heroin is another street drug for which there is a lot of word-of-mouth information but no research. For cocaine and marijuana, there are reports of good and bad side effects on sex. For heroin, almost all of the information shows that it has bad effects on sex. Two effects are the most common. One is a loss of desire in men and women. The other one is delayed ejaculation in men (Buffum, 1982; Rosen, 1991). As the effects of heroin wear off, men are likely to ejaculate too quickly. There are *no* reports that heroin might improve sex.

Alcohol and Sexual Functioning

The effects of alcohol on sex depend very much on many things. One is the amount of alcohol a person drinks. Another is the person's history of alcohol use. Still another is how much alcohol a person can tolerate. It is also important to understand that alcohol has two kinds of effects. These are acute (short-term) and chronic (long-term) effects (Buffum, 1982; Laumann, Gagnon, Michael, & Michaels, 1994; Rosen, 1991).

For most men and women, drinking alcohol makes them lose some of their inhibitions. This is an acute effect of alcohol. This effect often makes them feel an increase in sexual desire. Even though desire may increase, being able to perform may decrease with the more alcohol a person drinks (Buffum, 1982; Laumann et al., 1994; Rosen, 1991). The point that drinking affects a person's sexual behavior varies from one person to the next. It depends on a person's tolerance level. For some people, this level may be two drinks. For others, it may be 10 or more drinks. There are other possible acute effects. For men, it is not being able to get an erection. For women, it is not being able to have an orgasm. Some people report that they become more "horny" when they drink alcohol. There is evidence that this comes from their beliefs about what alcohol does, *not* from the alcohol itself (Buffum, 1982; Laumann et al., 1994; Rosen, 1991).

Drinking to excess and over a long period of time can have effects on sex. Chronic use may cause sex problems even when the person is not drinking. The chronic use of alcohol can cause liver disease and damage to a man's testicles. Both the liver and the testicles are crucial for a man. These organs make and recycle the male hormone testosterone. So, damage to the liver and testicles often causes the level of this hormone to drop. In severe cases, the level drops below normal. When it does, the man loses the desire for sex and has a problem with erections. The man can also start to develop breasts. This is called *gynecomasti* in men. All men and women have both male and female hormones in their bodies. When the testosterone level drops, the female hormones take over.

Women who are alcoholic may have problems with orgasms. They may also have irregular periods. These women may also have a problem in becoming pregnant.

Many men and women who abuse alcohol or other drugs often have sex problems once they have stopped the abuse. The reason for this seems to be purely psychological in nature. Once the person has given up the substance, he or she becomes much more aware of everything. Being more aware, the person often worries more, has more concern, and is more sensitive. So, the person is more watchful and more easily distracted. Because the person is more aware, he or she focuses more on performance. This focus decreases pleasure and so interferes even more with the process of sex. The person might have used drugs to deal with sex problems. Now, without the drugs, the person becomes painfully aware that the problems are still there.

The sexual problems faced by someone recovering from alcoholism or other drug abuse usually are temporary. Also, the person can usually work through the problems with a supportive partner. To guide some people through this process, specialized counseling by a physician or therapist can be helpful.

Are There Aphrodisiacs?

An *aphrodisiac* is a food or drug that is supposed to make a person want and enjoy sex more. Is there such a thing? The simple answer is *no*. Humans have long searched for potions or drugs that could make their sex lives better. This search for aphrodisiacs appeals to those who hope to overcome their own sex problems. It also appeals to those who hope to make someone else interested in sex. For instance, people still think that oysters and ground rhino horn can improve their sex performance and skills. So far, this belief has only reduced the number of rhinos and oysters. There is no proof that any food, drug, or vitamin has a "booster" effect on a person's sex life (Rosen & Ashton, 1993).

There are no foods or other substances that are *guaranteed* to help a person's sex life. However, some legally made drugs—not aphrodisiacs—may have a helpful effect. One of these is yohimbine. Doctors currently suggest it for men who have problems with erections (Carey & Johnson, in press). Studies with yohimbine are still going on. Also, many drug companies are looking into other drugs that might help with sex problems.

Coping With Medical Factors That Interfere With Sex

A chronic illness is a condition that will affect a person for an unknown period of time. A chronic illness may require a person to make changes in his or her sex life. The person may have to go through many changes before finding an acceptable one. Most of the time, a person stops having sex until the pain and discomfort decrease to a level he or she can bear. The person not only has to adjust to living with a chronic disease. The person must also deal with other changes and issues. The person might have to change his or her lifestyle or deal with depression and anxiety.

The impact that a chronic disease has on a person's sex life depends on many things. One is how satisfying sex was before the disease. Another is how flexible the person was in his or her approach to sex. There is a general rule of thumb. Someone who had a good sex life and an open mind about sex will likely have a good sex life after getting the disease. For someone who did not have a good sex life or an open mind about sex, his or her sex life will get even worse. That person will most likely take even less interest in sex or may avoid sex altogether.

A person who has an open mind about sex will be able to cope better with medical factors. This is so because he or she will be more willing to seek out sexual pleasure in a variety of ways. A person who thinks of sex as only intercourse will feel deprived if the illness gets in the way of intercourse. A person who has no other ways for sexual pleasure should try to find new ones.

Exploring other ways for sexual pleasure starts with deciding why you have sex. A chronic illness might require you to change the ways you have sex. Even so, you can still enjoy the function of sex—pleasure, love, trust, intimacy. This is important to understand. For instance, caressing your partner's genitals may not end up in intercourse. However, it may give both of you pleasure, show love and trust, and make you feel more intimate. If you are willing to explore other ways for sex, you are more likely to increase your overall pleasure from sex.

Exercise

For this exercise, use Worksheet 4.1. Record all substances that you have used. These include alcohol, drugs, and medicines. Also write down your feelings about whether they have enhanced or interfered with your sex life. Next, try to evaluate the basis for your belief. Has the substance always had the same effect when you used it? Were there other factors that could have also had effects on sex? If you have a partner, ask your partner to make a similar list. Then, discuss your lists.

Chapter 4 Review

Answer by filling in the correct word or by circling **T** (True) or **F** (False). Answers are provided in Appendix B.

1. Name a disease that can have a direct effect on a person's sexual functioning. _____

2. Name a disease or physical condition that can have an indirect effect on the process of sex. _____

3. Drugs used to treat depression are commonly linked to sex problems.   **T F**

4. Oysters eaten in large amounts can help your sex life.   **T F**

5. Research has shown that cocaine will help men have stronger erections.   **T F**

Worksheet 4.1. Substances and Their Effects on Sexual Behavior

Substance   Effects on Sexual Behavior

1. _____

2. _____

3. _____

4. _____

5. _____

Worksheet 4.1. Substances and Their Effects on Sexual Behavior

	Substance	Effects on Sexual Behavior
1.		
2.		
3.		
4.		
5.		

Chapter 5

Factors That Affect Sexual Arousal

How Does Sexual Arousal Happen?

In both men and women, sexual arousal is a combination of two things. One of these is a strong psychological attraction. Physical feelings are the other. Most of the time, the physical sensations cause a man to get an erection. In a woman, they cause vaginal wetness. Sexual arousal can occur when there are enough good, or positive, factors for sex. It is not an automatic process.

In fact, an available partner and the wish to have sex are not always enough to cause arousal. Sexual arousal is a little like sleep. The harder you try to make it happen, the more likely it will not happen. Many things have an effect on sexual arousal. You must understand these factors to know how or why arousal does or does not occur. Then, you need to figure out the ratio of positive to negative factors. If there are more positive factors, arousal is likely to occur. If there are more negative factors, arousal is not likely to occur.

A person can be aroused physically during sex even when he or she does not want to be. This can happen during sexual assault or abuse. The victim may become aroused and may even have an orgasm. This does not mean that the victim is enjoying the experience. It means only that there is enough stimulation to arouse the victim's body. The fear and anger that often go with sexual abuse may even make the arousal stronger. This is so because the body feels fear, anger, and sexual arousal in the same way. All of these cause increases in heart rate, blood pressure, and breathing rate. The signs of arousal in a person's body during abuse may confuse the victim. The body is aroused by something that frightens and repulses the victim.

Factors Affecting Your Sexual Arousal

Many factors can have an effect on sexual arousal. In general, they fall into three categories. One of these is biological. One is psychological, or how you think and feel. One has to do with issues between you and your partner and is called interpersonal.

Biological Factors

There are many physical factors that can have an effect the arousal. These include diseases and physical conditions that affect how you feel. They also include the effects of certain prescribed drugs and the abuse of alcohol and other drugs. How a disease, medicine, or drug affects sex cannot be predicted for any one person. Some factors, such as certain prescribed drugs, block the sex drive in the brain. Other factors affect how the body works. Biological factors may hinder the process of sex, but they do not have to stop it all the way. This is important to understand. Some people go on with their sex life even with negative physical factors. They can do this because the other factors for sex are very good. For example, a man with diabetes may have a problem getting an erection most of the time. Under special conditions, like a vacation, he can get a good erection. Figure 5.1 can help you understand this idea better.

This scale can help you understand how the positive and negative factors can affect sex. In sexual encounter, these factors interact to make sex good or not so good. They can tip the scale *for* or *against* sexual functioning. The balance of these factors, of course, can change. Sometimes the factors lead to satisfying sex. Sometimes they lead to sex that is not very satisfying. A sexual encounter should not be thought of as either all good or as all bad. Sex can be good even if it is not perfect or amazing. However, certain negative factors may be so severe that no kind of sex is possible. This can happen regardless of how many positive factors there are. For example, in a man with severe diabetes, very little blood flows to the penis. In such cases, the man cannot get an erection even if he is very aroused.

Psychological Factors

Psychological factors can also have an effect on the process of sex. The term *psychological* may not be exactly the right word. We do not mean "crazy" versus "normal." *Personal* might be a better term for factors that are not physical. Personal factors include self-esteem or how good you feel about yourself. They include a positive attitude toward sex and being "in the mood." Feeling good about yourself includes liking your body. This and having a good attitude toward sex are important for the process of sex. Perhaps you feel unsure of yourself, uneasy about sex, or depressed. In any of these cases, it is very hard to be sexually intimate with someone else. Another personal factor is being able to focus on pleasure and not on how you perform. Another one is being able to focus on

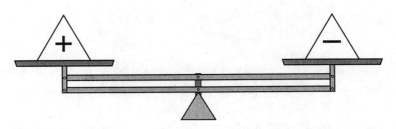

Psychological Factors	Good emotional health	Depression or PTSD
	Attraction toward partner	Lack of partner attraction
	Positive attitude toward partner	Negative attitude toward partner
	Positive sex attitude	Negative attitude toward sex
	Focus on pleasure	Focus on performance
	Newness	Routine, habit
	Good self-esteem	Poor self-esteem
	Comfortable environment for sex	Uncomfortable environment for sex
	Flexible attitude toward sex	Rigid, narrow attitude toward sex
Physical Factors	No smoking	Smoking
	No excess alcohol	Too much alcohol
	No medications that effect sex	Antihypertensive medication (heart)/Drugs
	Good physical health	Poor physical health
	Regular, appropriate exercise	Heart and blood-flow problems
	Good nutrition	Diabetes
	Successful Sexual Functioning	**Dysfunctional Sexual Functioning**

Figure 5.1.   **Positive and Negative Factors That Affect Sexual Functioning**

41

sexually pleasing thoughts. To enjoy sex, the person should not have thoughts about sex that are upsetting or thoughts that are not sexual.

Men, much more often than women, have thoughts that interfere with sex: Will I be able to get an erection? How well will I perform? Will my partner criticize me? Men also have thoughts that are not sexual, such as being worried about work. Sex is best when a person can focus on erotic, or sexy, images. If a woman lets her thoughts wander, she may have a problem with vaginal wetness. The physical setting and the timing of sex are other factors that can interfere with sex. They cause the person to have thoughts that are not sexual. These include the hour of day or night, the surroundings, and the degree of privacy. They also include the noise level and guests or relatives in the house.

Sex problems rarely have anything to do with being sane or insane. However, some psychological factors may get in the way of sex. Feeling depressed makes most men and women have little or no desire for sex. Being depressed can have physical effects. It usually slows down the body's functions such as heart rate and breathing rate. Sex speeds them up. So, it is harder for the body to respond sexually when a person is depressed.

There is another mental condition that may hinder sex. This is posttraumatic stress disorder (PTSD). Men and women who have had a severe trauma may have symptoms of this disorder. One symptom is constant worry about being hurt by others. When a person is overly vigilant, he or she is always "on guard." This can keep a person from focusing on the pleasant thoughts needed for sex. So, he or she is likely to have less desire for sex and a harder time becoming aroused.

Interpersonal Factors

Many interpersonal factors can have effects on your sex life. How well do you get along with your partner? How attractive is your partner to you? How comfortable is your partner with sex? How does your partner approach sex? Men seem to be less aware than women of how important partner factors can be. Many men expect to function even when there are very clear, adverse partner issues. Some seem to think having an available partner is all that counts. A partner's put-downs and lack of interest can surely interfere with sex. This is true even if the person is not aware of his or her own reactions. Men tell us that their partners say to them, "Hurry up and get it over with." These same men ask, "Why don't I have erections?" or "Why don't I feel turned on?"

There is one more important factor that has an effect on arousal. This is a basic physical attraction to your partner. Just because your partner is available and you love and respect him or her does not mean you will be aroused. This is true for both men and women. Arousal for a man (erection) and for a woman (vaginal wetness) depends on the same thing. The level of erotic excitement must be high enough.

Understanding the Reasons for Sex

Most men and women do not think much about why they have sex. Most of the time, people say they have sex "because it feels good" or "because I am in love." Reasons for sex, however, may differ greatly. These reasons depend on whether your partner is a "new" partner or a "familiar" one. A new partner is one you have been involved with for 6 months or less. A familiar partner is one you know very well. In a relationship with a new partner, there are two important reasons for having sex. These reasons are physical attraction and newness. In a long-term relationship, other reasons for sex come into play from time to time. For instance, a man and woman in a committed relationship may have sex to have children. Couples also have sex to show their love for each other, to make up after an argument, or just to have fun.

The reasons for having sex have an effect on how satisfying the sex is. One reason for having sex may make the sex very good physically. Another reason for having sex may make the sex very good in a psychological way. It is important to understand that sex may be more—or less—pleasurable. Some people who seek help for a sex problem expect sex to be intense and amazing every time. It is unrealistic to expect this. Even so, when the sex does not reach this high level, some people become unhappy or angry. Others want to withdraw and to shut off their desires for sex entirely.

People can avoid problems if they remind themselves that the reasons for sex may differ from time to time. They should also remember that sex will be more or less intense and great from one time to the next. Also, the firmness of a man's erection and the amount of wetness in a woman will differ from time to time. *All of these things are normal.*

Understanding Positive Factors for Sex

For most people, there are two conditions that are essential for sex. These are privacy and a setting that is free from distraction. Beyond these two, the ideas about good conditions for sex vary from one person to the next. Every person has conditions that make sex more appealing and put him or her "in the mood." Every person also has conditions that make sex less appealing and that do not put him or her in the mood. Everyone has likes and dislikes that differ. Some people like candles and mirrors. Some like the lights off. Some want to have sex in the morning, others at night. Some people want to take a shower before, and some do not.

Problems can come up when a person does not think about all the things that can affect sexual pleasure. Many people think that sex will be great in spite of the situation or conditions. They think if a man or a woman is "willing and able," sex should be a good experience. A willing and able partner does not guarantee good sex. Sex is likely to be occurring in situations that could be much better. Most couples can improve sex. They can bring together the right conditions, or they can alternate conditions to suit each other. Bad problems come up when couples are not flexible enough to work on their differences.

Understanding Negative Factors for Sex

There are also conditions that are not favorable for sex. These are anything that does not make the setting comfortable or that keeps a person from getting aroused. An unfavorable factor is anything that gets a person "out of the mood." Examples are things that take away a person's attention or that create worry. These are psychological factors that do not favor sex.

So, it makes good "sex" sense to increase the factors that enhance sex and to decrease the factors that interfere with sex. This guideline seems like common sense. However, couples often have problems because they try to have sex under the worst of conditions. For example, they have sex when they are not in the mood, or they have sex right before the kids come home.

Aging and Sexuality

Men and women often ask about the effects of age on sexual functioning. Does sex stop at a certain age? This is the most common age-related question. Another frequent question is "Does sex peak at a certain age?" The answer to both of these questions is that age does affect sex to some degree. This is true for both men and women. However, being able to perform or enjoy sex does not stop at any age. Also, sex does not "peak" at any age. There are factors that are far more important than age for making sex great or disappointing. Another is how good your relationship is with your partner. Another is how attracted you are to your partner and your partner to you. Still another is freedom from worry and from other factors that can interfere with sex.

Although age alone does not determine how good sex will be, it does bring about some notable changes in sex. For men, the most notable change has to do with erections. As a man ages, he has fewer erections just from thinking about sex or seeing something sexy. Some men think they are impotent because they no longer get such erections. This is not true. Such erections can certainly occur at any age. However, most men notice a change in their late thirties or forties. In general, as a man ages, he needs more direct touching of the penis to get an erection.

Another change for men is the time it takes to become aroused again after an orgasm. The older a man gets, the longer it takes. The time after an orgasm is called the *refractory period*. This period for a man in his teens or twenties may be only minutes. A man in his sixties may take an hour or more before he can get another erection.

Finally, the time that a man takes to ejaculate changes as he gets older. As a rule, young men always ejaculate very quickly. In general, older men take longer. Other factors also affect the time that it takes a man to ejaculate. These are discussed in Chapter 6.

Aging also produces some changes in sex for women. As with men, women may also need more direct touching of the genitals to become aroused. Also, it may take longer to become aroused. As women enter menopause, they may notice another change. This is a sharp decrease in vaginal wetness during sex. Intercourse may become less comfortable and may even cause pain. Lubricants or estrogen replacement therapy may help. But for both men and women, there are more important factors than age. These are the circumstances under which sex occurs and general health.

The changes that occur for both men and women are normal and should not stop sex at any age. What usually interferes with sex as a person gets older is a decline in health.

Exercise

This exercise will help you pinpoint those factors that will make the conditions for sex better. Use Worksheet 5.1 to make a list of your "likes" about settings that enhance good sex. Think of time that you enjoyed sex the most. In this way, you may be able to find many positive factors. Try to pinpoint physical factors such as time of day, place, and comfort. Try to think of personal factors such as your mood, being able to relax, and how aroused you were.

If you have a partner, ask your partner to make a list also. Then set aside time to talk about what each of you likes and dislikes. Try to compromise if there are too many differences.

Chapter 5 Review

Answer by circling **T** (True) or **F** (False). Answers are provided in Appendix B.

1. Anger, fear, and sexual arousal all affect the body in much the same ways. T F

2. Once a man has diabetes, he is no longer able to have sex. T F

3. A focus on performance during sex can help you do better. T F

4. Being overly vigilant often comes after a bad trauma, and it can interfere with sex. T F

5. With a partner who is willing and able, you should always feel sexual pleasure. T F

Worksheet 5.1. Positive Factors Affecting Sexual Experiences

Environmental Factors:

1. _____

2. _____

3. _____

4. _____

5. _____

Personal or Psychological Factors:

1. _____

2. _____

3. _____

4. _____

5. _____

Worksheet 5.1. Positive Factors Affecting Sexual Experiences

Environmental Factors:

1. _____

2. _____

3. _____

4. _____

5. _____

Personal or Psychological Factors:

1. _____

2. _____

3. _____

4. _____

5. _____

Chapter 6

Problems With Ejaculation in Men and With Orgasm in Men and Women

Useful Information About Ejaculation

Almost every man has had a time when he ejaculated sooner than he wanted to. Some men have had the experience of not being able to ejaculate at all. Some men have had times of being able to do so only after very long periods of stimulation. It will help to know some basic things about the process of ejaculation. The process is really very hard for men to control. Many factors can affect the timing with which a man ejaculates during sex. These include age, frequency of sex, and degree of arousal.

Age and Frequency of Sex

In general, the younger a man is, the more quickly he will ejaculate. This pattern likely has to do with many factors. These are good physical health, the newness of sex, and fewer chances for sex when a man does not have a steady partner. The more often a man ejaculates, the longer he may "last" (keep an erection) during sex. For instance, a man who has had sex twice in the same night will likely have more control during the second time. A man who has not had sex for a week or more may not have as much control as one who has had sex three times a week. The link between how often a man has sex and his control of ejaculating is open to debate. Research about this has not given clear results (see Suggested Readings for more information).

Degree of Sexual Arousal

The more intense his arousal is, the more quickly a man will ejaculate. The factors we just talked about may surely have an effect on a man's ejaculation. However, there is no sure way to guarantee control for a man. Like most human behaviors, the pattern of ejaculating will differ from one man to the next. Every man is different from all other men in his physical makeup. This difference will cause one man to ejaculate sooner than another man. This is true in spite of other factors.

Most men and their partners do not understand this fact. When a man ejaculates too soon, the partners may think that one or the other or both are doing something wrong. The same is true when the man takes too long to ejaculate. Often the result is anger, blame, and anxiety. Many people have unreal ideas about how long a man should be able to last. They have these ideas because of "locker-room bragging," folklore, and porno movies. Research has been done on the time a man takes to ejaculate after penetration. The results show that the average time is between 2 and 8 minutes for most men (Crooks & Baur, 1993; McCarthy, 1988; Wincze & Carey, 1991). There are methods that may help some men gain better control of ejaculation. These are outlined in Chapter 10 but are not the most important factors. The best way to deal with concerns about ejaculation is for men and their partners to learn and share the facts. In this way, both partners can have realistic expectations.

Many drugs used to treat mental problems can affect the speed of ejaculation (Meston & Gorzalka, 1992). For instance, some drugs used to treat depression can slow down ejaculation. Such drugs are for the treatment of other problems, not for slowing down ejaculation. The effect of slowing down ejaculation is a side effect. Because it is a side effect, its use for this cannot be predicted. Ointments that deaden the nerves in the penis have been used to treat men with ejaculation problems. However, the benefits are open to debate. The ointment may decrease pleasure rather than give the man more control. You should ask your doctor for more information (also see Suggested Readings for more information).

Useful Information About Orgasms in Men

Most of the time, orgasms for men occur at the same time as ejaculation. However, a man can ejaculate and not have an orgasm. Also, a man can have an orgasm and not ejaculate. Even if a man does not have an erection, he can still ejaculate and have an orgasm. Factors that interfere with sex can keep a man from ejaculating. They can also keep a man from having an orgasm and getting an erection. They can also disturb the common sequence of response.

Some men think that every orgasm should be very intense. If it is not, they are surprised, upset, and worried. A man can have very mild to very intense orgasms. The most important factor that affects the intensity is how aroused a man feels. The more aroused a man is, the more intense the orgasm will be. The factors that affect orgasm most are age, how well the man knows his sex partner, and state of mind. In general, the younger a man is, the more intense his orgasm will be. As we said before, the age of a man may also affect the pattern of ejaculation.

In general, if a man is with the same partner for a long time, the intensity of his orgasm may decrease. There are some changes that may help increase the intensity. For example, a new setting, like a hotel on vacation, can make sex more exciting. A new approach, such as a new sexual position, might make the orgasm more intense.

If a man is depressed or worried, then his orgasm may be very mild. It might even be stopped entirely. The opposite is also true. If he is happy and free of worry, he may have a more intense orgasm during sex.

The drugs that have an effect on ejaculation also seem to hinder orgasm. There is no prescribed or street drug that can guarantee more intense orgasms. Some prescribed drugs may stop the ejaculation but not the orgasm.

Useful Information About Orgasms in Women

Orgasms in both men and women can range from very mild to very intense. The factors that work for or against orgasm for men also work the same way for women. Orgasms for women do differ from those of men in many ways, however.

First, women generally do not reach orgasm as easily as men do. For women, experience seems to count. The more experience with sex that a woman has, the more likely she is to have an orgasm during sex. Experience seems to help a woman to learn what type of stimulation is best for her. It is usual for a woman to learn to have an orgasm one way and not another way. For instance, a woman may have an orgasm by intercourse but not oral sex. The way a woman reaches an orgasm may be a matter of learned behavior. It may simply be a matter of preference. One way is not more right or more wrong than any other.

Second, women are able to recover more quickly than men after an orgasm. Women are physically able to have many orgasms in a row. This is call multiple orgasms. In general, men need a period of time to recover between orgasms. This period for men is the *refractory period* and tends to last longer as a man gets older. Some young men have reported having multiple orgasms. However, they are much more common in women.

There may be a third difference between orgasms in women and those in men. Some researchers believe that there are two distinct types of orgasms for women. One type comes from stimulating the clitoris. The other type comes from stimulation during intercourse (Laumann et al., 1994).

Fourth, women do not always have to have an orgasm during sex to feel satisfied. For most men, orgasm tends to be the goal of sex. So, when orgasm does not occur, a man may feel unfulfilled or that he has failed. This same feeling is less frequently true for women. Although women may desire and enjoy orgasm, it is not their only goal. Sharing, touching, and being desired are also very important to women. Men often do not understand this. Men think they have failed if their partners do not have an orgasm, even when the partners say they feel satisfied.

Exercise

Think of the time when you have had your most intense orgasm. Compare this to a time when you have had a very mild orgasm. Use Worksheet 6.1 to list the factors that might have added to or taken from those times. This will give you some idea of what to expect from your sexual encounters.

Chapter 6 Review

Answer by circling **T** (True) or **F** (False). Answers are provided in Appendix B.

1. Men are able to control the time it takes to ejaculate by strong willpower. **T   F**

2. Quick ejaculation is most common in younger men. **T   F**

3. Men's orgasms are always the same, but women's orgasms vary in intensity. **T   F**

4. If a woman says that she does not need to have an orgasm during sex to be satisfied, she is lying. **T   F**

5. Women are capable of having many orgasms in a row. **T   F**

Worksheet 6.1. Factors Affecting Sexual Experiences

Factors that make sex better for you:

1. _____

2. _____

3. _____

4. _____

5. _____

Factors that take away from your enjoying sex:

1. _____

2. _____

3. _____

4. _____

5. _____

Worksheet 6.1. Factors Affecting Sexual Experiences

Factors that make sex better for you:

1. _____

2. _____

3. _____

4. _____

5. _____

Factors that take away from your enjoying sex:

1. _____

2. _____

3. _____

4. _____

5. _____

Chapter 7

Problems With Pain and Discomfort During Sexual Penetration

Useful Information About Penetration and Pain

Women are much more likely than men to complain of pain or discomfort during intercourse. In fact, men rarely have such complaints. If a man has constant pain in the penis or testicles during or after sex, he should see a doctor. Such pain is almost always a medical problem. However, many women have had pain and discomfort during sex at one time or another. For women, pain or discomfort during or after sex may have many different causes. These can be a medical problem, stress, or anxiety.

Infections in the urinary tract are the most common causes of pain linked to sex. This is true for both men and women. Some drugs used to treat depression and other mental problems may be linked to pain during orgasm. Again, this is true for both men and women. There are other causes of pain during sex for women. One is a condition called *endometriosis*. It causes tissue from the lining of the uterus to grow outside the uterus. The lack of vaginal wetness that is common when a woman goes through menopause also can cause pain.

Both men and women can have pain during sex for no medical reason. This kind of pain is called *dyspareunia*. There is also pain that follows sex that has no medical causes. There are several causes for pain during or after sex. These are fear of sex, low desire for sex, lack of arousal, or past sexual trauma. A person who links sex with pain often avoids sex. This can add to the problem. Couples often think of sex in an all-or-nothing way. So, they avoid sex entirely or try to have complete intercourse every time. The solution to the problem is a gradual approach to sex over a period of time. With this approach, penetration is increased little by little over time. A good rule to remember is that behaviors can be broken down into simpler steps. Solving a problem one little step at a time makes the problem less overwhelming. This approach is very helpful for solving sex problems linked to stress or anxiety. Chapter 10 has more detailed solutions for dealing with pain during sex.

Useful Information for Women Who Cannot Tolerate Any Penetration

For some women, penetration during sex is not possible at all. The reason is that the muscles in the vagina tighten up. For many of these women, this happens even in situations that have nothing to do with sex. For instance, it can happen when the woman tries to insert a tampon. This condition is called *vaginismus*. Some women who have it have never been able to bear any penetration at all. For other women, it occurs only after they have had intercourse that was painful.

Most men and women do not know much about vaginismus and dyspareunia. The effects of these conditions can frustrate and embarrass a woman and her partner. The problem is made even worse by the blame and anger that often go along with them. A woman and her partner sometimes think the solution is just a matter of trying harder. This is not true. Most women very much want to be able to have sex, but their bodies will not let them. The causes of vaginismus may be the same as those for dyspareunia. The ways for dealing with them are the same and are outlined in more detail in Chapter 10.

Exercise

To solve the problems pain and penetration, take a gradual approach to sex. Allow sex to stop at any time without anger or guilt. If you are working with a partner, talk to your partner about the need for this approach. The two of you must come to a comfortable and trusting agreement before you start to work on the problem. The ways of doing this are outlined in Chapter 10.

Chapter 7 Review

Answer by circling **T** (True) or **F** (False). Answers are provided in Appendix B.

1. It is common for men to have pain during sex.   T   F

2. Women who have pain during sex are usually not trying hard enough.   T   F

3. The lack of vaginal wetness is common in women who have gone through menopause.   T   F

4. Infections in the urinary tract are the most common cause of pain during sex for men and for women.   T   F

5. When a woman cannot stand any penetration at all, it is called vaginismus.   T   F

Chapter 8

The Relationship With a Sexual Partner as the First Step in Treatment

Importance of a Good Partner Relationship

Treatment for almost all sex problems must start with working on good partner relations. A couple might get along well in most other areas of their relationship. However, they must view and approach a sex problem as a shared one if they are to overcome it. The couple must put aside blame for the problem in order to reach a solution. This "couple" approach to a sex problem is important whether or not the couple are married.

Some people with a sex problem ignore the importance of the relationship as a whole. They think that a partner who is available and willing is all that is needed for sex to occur. However, there are many other important factors that can help or interfere with your sex life. We pointed these out in Chapter 4. This chapter talks about the things in a partnership that lead to a satisfying sex life.

It is true that sometimes a couple dislike each other and do not get along and still have a great sex life together. This is true in spite of major problems. It is also true that a couple can love each other deeply and get along very well and still have an awful sex life. Ideally, the person one loves is the person one has great sex with. This does not always happen.

Couples who have been together only a short time may find that there are two factors that are the most important ones for sex. These are the chance for sex and the physical attraction ("chemistry") they have for each other. For a new couple, the newness itself can cover up basic differences between them. However, even a new partnership can have sex problems. You might feel a lot of pressure from the relationship. Also, your new partner might remind you of something negative, such as someone whom you do not like. It is easy for such an interfering thought to shut off the desire for sex and result in a sex problem.

There are many factors that can affect the sex life of a couple who are in a long-term relationship. These have to do with the personalities of the two people. Here are the ones that interfere with a couple's sexual desire most of the time:

- One partner wants to control. The other partner is silent but resentful.

- Both partners wish to control. They often clash over even minor issues.

- Partners do not have skills for communicating or for solving problems.

- The partners drift apart because they have no common interests and values.

- A partner may not be able to resolve anger about past events, drug abuse, or conflicts.

Many other interpersonal factors may lead to sex problems. However, these five factors are the ones that happen again and again. They lead to anger, lack of respect, and distance between the two people. When such factors exist, couples tend to avoid sex and go longer and longer without having sex.

Some couples get along very well and do not deal with these kinds of interpersonal factors. However, they still may have sex problems. The man may have a problem with erections, or the woman may have one with having an orgasm. Most of the time, the problems come from a person's attitudes toward sex or from not feeling secure. For the most part, they do not come from interpersonal conflict. You must be able to understand your own feelings and to talk openly with your partner. Being able to do these two things will help you to pinpoint the source of the sex problem and to work toward a way of solving it.

What Are Your Feelings Toward Your Partner?

People often report that they have bad feelings toward their partners. When asked what keeps them in the relationship, they say "because I love her" or "because I love him." The concept of love is the basic building block for most long-term relationships. However, for many couples, real love often is not present. People frequently claim to "love" their partners. At the same time, they admit to many things that hurt the relationship. They might have been angry toward the partner for a very long time. They may have no interests in common. Their long-term goals may be very different. They may not be able to talk to each other or do not care about the other's feelings. So, what is going on? What do people in such relationships really mean when they say they love their partners?

There are many possible meanings behind such statements about love. Some people just mean that they put up with the partner and that it is a "familiar" relationship. Others mean that even with many bad parts of their partnership, they have some good feelings toward their partners. They feel sexually attracted to or feel sorry for their partner. Others may mean that there are family or financial reasons to stay together. They label these "obligations" as love.

Clearly, then, people can mean many different things when they say "love." To pinpoint the good and bad aspects of a relationship, it is best not to use the term *love*. We are not saying you should not use the term *love* to express your feelings toward your partner. Instead, we are saying that in trying to understand your feelings, using the word *love* does not help. In fact, using the word *love* to explain your true feelings sometimes hinders rather than helps. It may be more helpful for you to explain your true feelings for your partner in terms of other emotions. You can do this by answering the questions in Worksheet 8.1. These questions deal with possible partner-related factors that may interfere with your sex life. Your answers can help you pinpoint emotional factors that may be having an effect on your sex life.

Did you check "Often" or "Almost Always" on any one of the questions in Worksheet 8.1? If so, your sex problem is likely partner related. A partner factor does not rule out other possible problems, such as a medical problem. A partner factor means that your relationship with your partner is part of your sex problem. The source of your strong bad feelings toward your partner could be any of the factors talked about at the start of this chapter.

Did you check "Never" or "Almost Never" on all five questions? If so, it is not likely that your sex problem is partner related. Your problem is likely a medical or personal one.

Important Sexual Behaviors and Attitudes of Partners

We just talked about common conflicts between you and your partner that could cause strong bad feelings toward your partner. These feelings, in turn, can interfere with your sex life together. Approaches to sex and attitudes toward sex can also keep you from enjoying sex. These include not being very interested in sex or placing too much importance on sex. They also include an approach that is narrow minded or rigid. All of these can cause sex problems, especially for couples in long-term partnerships.

A Lack of Enthusiasm for Sex

Often one partner in a couple has little or no enthusiasm for sex. The other partner may say, "My partner tells me to hurry up and get it over with." "My partner just lies there and hardly moves." These are common complaints. Your partner's lack of enthusiasm for sex will surely affect your being able to perform. This is true because your partner's sexual excitement is a big part of your own excitement.

Rigid or Narrow-Minded Approach to Sex

Variety truly is the spice of life when it comes to long-term sexual partnerships. Couples who are not very creative or willing to try new things will, in time, lose interest in sex. They may even develop sex problems. For many couples, sex includes little or no foreplay. They focus all interest on intercourse. Some couples have never touched each other's genitals. Some have never tried new positions for intercourse. These couples are limiting the pleasure they could have from sex. They are also at risk for sex problems and physical isolation. On the other hand, other couples have enjoyed many ways of giving each other sexual pleasure. Because of this, they are better prepared to deal with a problem with intercourse if one occurs. These couples give and receive pleasure in a number of ways. This keeps them feeling physically intimate and close to each other.

Attaching Too Much Importance to Sex

Sex is an important part of many people's lives, but some place too much importance on sex. They view any sex problem almost as seriously as they would view a fatal illness. For some people, a sex problem means they are no longer masculine or feminine. Others view any sex problem as a sure sign that the relationship is over. Most of the time, depression or extreme tension goes along with such views. People with these views almost never enjoy sex in a relaxed way. They focus too much on how they perform and not enough on fun, being creative, and satisfaction.

Can You Communicate Openly About Sex With Your Partner?

If you have a sex problem, the first and most important step is to discuss the problem with your partner. This is true for a problem that is caused by inter-personal factors. It is true for problems that stem from attitudes and behaviors about sex. For most people, this is easier said than done. A couple often do not talk about a problem with the relationship or their sex life. If they do talk, the discussion is often awkward. When couples do not talk, misunderstandings are much more likely. It has been shown that talking really does help. Couples can get ride of a lot tension and can sometimes even correct a sex problem just by talking about it.

On the other hand, discussing problems about the relationship or sex life can be poor and useless. A couple must follow a good communication plan. Keep in mind that you are trying to understand each other's feelings and the ways you affect each other's behavior. If you use discussions to blame one another, they will be useless—or worse—harmful to the relationship.

Developing Better Communication With Your Partner

Most couples who have a hard time communicating try to do so at the wrong times. Couples may try to talk when one person is leaving for work or has just walked in the door. Distractions and interruptions can ruin the chance of the discussion being a good one. On the other hand, couples with good communication skills set aside time for talking. They also make sure there will not be any distractions. They unplug telephones, turn off the television, and make sure the children are occupied. They also make sure they have plenty of time. Worksheet 8.2 lists other good communication skills. On this worksheet, check off the sender and receiver skills that you think you usually use. The skills you do *not* check off are the ones you can try to improve.

If you use these sender and receiver skills, you can make communication much better. Also, discussions are less likely to turn into arguing. Often, the focus of therapy is on bad problems in communication and the need for better skills. Even partners who have been together for many years fail when they try to talk about important topics. These couples find that coaching from a therapist on these skills can help a great deal.

Are You Currently Without a Sexual Partner?

Many single people who do not have a steady partner and who fear failure in sex come for therapy. They may not socialize because they do not wish to set themselves up for failure or embarrassment. Most of the time, avoidance makes them have even more fear. This fear, in turn, leads to more avoidance.

We have a strong recommendation for single people who do not have a steady partner and who fear sex. They should go about socializing and becoming intimate one step at a time. Many of them may need a lot of support and encouragement to start going out again. Often, they continue not to socialize because of false beliefs. Some men, for instance, think that if a woman shows an interest in having sex, then they must attempt sex. So, rather than fail, they avoid. Some women may think that all men are interested in them only for sex and that they will always be pressured for sex.

Remind yourself that you are in charge of choosing who you go out with. Also, it is perfectly okay to state to a potential partner that you are not ready for sex. In fact, you should not keep going out with someone if you feel pressured and if you feel the person is not sensitive to your needs. You should look for someone who attracts you and who has interests in common with you. The person should have a flexible and accepting view of sex. Avoid people who have very strong, fixed ideas about what is right and wrong in sex. Keep in mind that a person who is rigid about sex is likely to develop sex problems or to add to them. A good sex partner is someone who is relaxed, knowledgeable, and open-minded about sex.

Exercise

This chapter has tried to help you to understand the importance of good partner relations. It has also tried to help you pinpoint areas in a partnership that are prone to problems. Worksheet 8.1 covers partner factors that can possibly interfere with sex. Worksheet 8.2 lists good communication skills. Review your responses on these worksheets. In this way, you can pinpoint areas that need work. Chapters 2 and 3 suggested that you set aside a special time to discuss important issues with your partner. Use this time now to talk about each of the points that you identified in Worksheets 8.1 and 8.2.

Whether or not you have a partner, you can practice the communication skills listed in Worksheet 8.2. Be aware of these skills when talking to people you meet during the day. For example, use them with relatives, people at work, and friends. At the end of each day, review the list from Worksheet 8.2. How did you do on each skill? By practicing daily, you will find that these skills become second nature.

Chapter 8 Review

Answer by circling **T** (True) or **F** (False). Answers are provided in Appendix B.

1. Couples who are having sex problems are not in love.   **T F**

2. If you focus on intercourse and exclude other behaviors from sex, you will have better sex.   **T F**

3. Couples with poor communication often try to talk at the wrong times.   **T F**

4. Being honest and direct when you communicate will cause hurt feelings.   **T F**

5. Single people who have sex problems should not socialize until they solve their problems.   **T F**

Worksheet 8.1. Possible Partner-Related Factors That May Interfere With Sexual Relations

1. Do you have strong feelings of anger toward your partner?

    Never   Almost Never   Sometimes   Often   Almost Always

2. Do you not really care about your partner's feelings?

    Never   Almost Never   Sometimes   Often   Almost Always

3. Do you feel tense or anxious around your partner?

    Never   Almost Never   Sometimes   Often   Almost Always

4. Do you feel depressed or "down" around your partner?

    Never   Almost Never   Sometimes   Often   Almost Always

5. Do you feel little or no sexual attraction toward your partner?

    Never   Almost Never   Sometimes   Often   Almost Always

Worksheet 8.1. Possible Partner-Related Factors That May Interfere With Sexual Relations

1. Do you have strong feelings of anger toward your partner?

   Never   Almost Never   Sometimes   Often   Almost Always

2. Do you not really care about your partner's feelings?

   Never   Almost Never   Sometimes   Often   Almost Always

3. Do you feel tense or anxious around your partner?

   Never   Almost Never   Sometimes   Often   Almost Always

4. Do you feel depressed or "down" around your partner?

   Never   Almost Never   Sometimes   Often   Almost Always

5. Do you feel little or no sexual attraction toward your partner?

   Never   Almost Never   Sometimes   Often   Almost Always

Worksheet 8.2. Positive Communication Skills

If the statement describes what you do, place a check mark in the box.

Sender Skills (The *sender* is the person who wants to talk about an issue or problem.)

1. Stay with the topic you wish to discuss. Do not bring into the discussion old topics or topics that are not related, which sidetrack the issue. ☐

2. Point out behaviors you would like changed and avoid general statements. For example, do not say, "You need a better attitude." Instead, say, "I wish you would focus more on the good things I do and less on what you feel I do wrong." ☐

3. Be honest and direct. Don't leave your partner guessing about what you mean. ☐

4. Talk about your feelings or thoughts without accusing or name calling. ☐

5. Talk in an adult way and do not "talk down" to your partner, as if he or she were a child. Be polite and talk to your partner as you would to anyone you respect. ☐

6. Do not use words like "never" or "always." Always try to use words that reflect a real situation or behavior. Doing this will give more meaning to your statements, and your partner will be more likely to listen to what you have to say. ☐

7. If you must say something negative to your partner, try to be helpful and not hurtful. Point out some good behaviors about your partner when you are also pointing out bad ones. In this way, you address your partner's behavior rather than his or her whole personality. ☐

Receiver Skills (The *receiver* is the person with whom the sender wants to have the discussion.)

1. Use behaviors that show you are interested. These include eye contact, nods of agreement, and body posture. ☐

2. Control over your own behavior until it is your turn to talk. You do not interrupt or make faces. ☐

3. You make sure you understand what the sender is saying. To do this, say back in your own words statements that were unclear to you. ☐

4. Read the sender's nonverbal cues and respond to them. These are facial expressions, gestures, and other body language. For instance, you say, "You are frowning and seem upset." This shows you are paying attention and are sensitive to the sender's feelings. ☐

Worksheet 8.2. Positive Communication Skills

If the statement describes what you do, place a check mark in the box.

Sender Skills (The *sender* is the person who wants to talk about an issue or problem.)

1. Stay with the topic you wish to discuss. Do not bring into the discussion old topics or topics that are not related, which sidetrack the issue. ☐

2. Point out behaviors you would like changed and avoid general statements. For example, do not say, "You need a better attitude." Instead, say, "I wish you would focus more on the good things I do and less on what you feel I do wrong." ☐

3. Be honest and direct. Don't leave your partner guessing about what you mean. ☐

4. Talk about your feelings or thoughts without accusing or name calling. ☐

5. Talk in an adult way and do not "talk down" to your partner, as if he or she were a child. Be polite and talk to your partner as you would to anyone you respect. ☐

6. Do not use words like "never" or "always." Always try to use words that reflect a real situation or behavior. Doing this will give more meaning to your statements, and your partner will be more likely to listen to what you have to say. ☐

7. If you must say something negative to your partner, try to be helpful and not hurtful. Point out some good behaviors about your partner when you are also pointing out bad ones. In this way, you address your partner's behavior rather than his or her whole personality. ☐

Receiver Skills (The *receiver* is the person with whom the sender wants to have the discussion.)

1. Use behaviors that show you are interested. These include eye contact, nods of agreement, and body posture. ☐

2. Control over your own behavior until it is your turn to talk. You do not interrupt or make faces. ☐

3. You make sure you understand what the sender is saying. To do this, say back in your own words statements that were unclear to you. ☐

4. Read the sender's nonverbal cues and respond to them. These are facial expressions, gestures, and other body language. For instance, you say, "You are frowning and seem upset." This shows you are paying attention and are sensitive to the sender's feelings. ☐

Chapter 9

Working With a Partner To Master Your Sexual Problem

Identifying Common Goals

By now, you and your partner should have a good understanding of the nature of your sex problem and of its causes. You might also have solved most or all of your sex problems by having done all of the reading and exercises. Some people may have additional work to do. Chapter 7 explained what is involved in working on solutions. Some solutions are simple. Others require a great deal of work and emotional involvement. You and your partner have to decide how much time and energy you are willing to give to improve your sex life. Keep in mind that making your sex life better does not necessarily mean making it what it was before. It may mean adjusting to certain limits. It may also mean agreeing with your partner about a new sex pattern that fulfills and pleases both of you. This pattern may be different from the one you had before, but it can still be very rewarding. In this chapter, we review the crucial elements for solving a sex problem when you are working with a partner.

Setting Aside Quality Time

To agree on goals for you and your sex partner and to reach those goals, you must spend priority time with each other. Doing this is essential for sexual health. We have made this point in previous chapters. Once you and your partner commit to this, you have taken the most important step toward making your sex life better.

Identifying Conditions That Help Make Sex Satisfying

Sex, like sleep, requires special conditions for it to occur and be enjoyable. Many men and women often overlook this fact. Expectation alone does not guarantee that sex will occur or that you will enjoy it. This does not mean you have to make complex plans. It does mean you need to be aware of what works best for you and for your partner. Being aware can help you avoid negative conditions and take advantage of favorable ones. Chapter 5 explained these conditions.

Having the Right Attitude

The most important factor in solving your sex problem is for you and your partner to see it as a shared problem. It requires you to work together on common goals and to agree on causes and solutions. Sex problems can be very hard to solve. They may be impossible to solve if you and your partner do not agree on goals, causes, or solutions. Blaming does not help. Again, you and your partner must take the view of working together on a shared problem. It is obviously very hard not to blame when the blame has existed for a long time. Blame is often based on misunderstanding. You will need to get rid of blame. To do so, you must be open to new information and a new way of looking at your problem. Despite how your sex problem started, you must work on solving it with an open mind and with cooperation.

Perhaps you are single and you are avoiding relationships because of your sex problem. If so, you must find a partner who will help you to develop a healthy sexuality. Do not put more pressure on yourself by choosing a partner who is not sensitive to your problem. You are more likely to overcome a sex problem when your partner has an open attitude toward sex. Such a person can give and receive pleasure from sex in many ways and does not view sex as intercourse only. There are many potential partners for you. After a few dates, if you feel pressure or think the person you are dating is rigid about sex, then find someone else. It is perfectly okay and smart today to put off sex until you know your partner really well. Do not hesitate or be afraid to say that you do not want to rush into something sexual. If the person you are with becomes angry, find someone else.

Working With a Step-By-Step Approach To Master Your Sexual Problem

We have stressed that if you work steadily and take a step-by-step approach to your sex problem, you will enjoy sex more. In summary, this Workbook has guided you through the following steps:

1. Learn about sex problems in general and begin to assess your problems (Chapters 1–4).

2. Learn the important information about your sex problem (Chapters 5–7).

3. Master your problem by working with your partner. Then prevent slipping back by forming plans to deal with slips and to get back on track (Chapters 8–12).

It is important for your partner to be aware of these steps and to work with you on each step. This Workbook is set up so that you get the most benefit by completing each step before going on to the next. You and your partner have to work patiently. You must be thorough in order to solve your sex problems and to prevent slipping or developing new ones.

Exercise

With your partner, review the sexual goals you have reached and discuss your plans for reaching any goals that remain. You should agree on other goals and plans before you take any further steps. You may agree on some goals and and not agree on others. It is worthwhile to go ahead as long as you agree on at least one goal and on one way of reaching it.

Chapter 9 Review

Answer by circling **T** (True) or **F** (False). Answers are provided in Appendix B.

1. The goal in working on a sex problem is always to make sex what it used to be.   **T F**

2. A key element in solving your problem is setting aside time for you and your partner.   **T F**

3. If the chance for sex occurs, you should take advantage of it.   **T F**

4. Most of the time, sex problems are the fault of one of the partners in a relationship.   **T F**

5. If you are single, you should avoid going out until you solve your sex problem.   **T F**

Chapter 10

Mastering Your Sexual Problem

Putting Together All of the Information You Have Learned So Far

By now, you should have learned some very specific information about your sex problem. From each chapter and exercise, you have gained a great deal of understanding about your sex problem. You have perhaps already found some solutions. So far, you should have added to what you know about human sexuality and common sex problems. You should also have learned how to assess your own sex problem and how to begin some work on it. This chapter should help you keep working toward the solution to your problem.

Most sex problems have a combination of causes. To solve your sex problem, you must pinpoint all of the specific causes or sources of your problem. Then you must work on solutions to those causes. The fastest and surest way of solving your sex problem is to follow the guidelines designed just for your problem.

Identifying Your Sexual Problem

The title of Worksheet 10.1 is "Common Causes or Sources of Sex Problems." You can use it as a quick checklist to pinpoint the source of your problem as you read this chapter. This checklist is not a complete list of all sex problems. However, it does list the sources of sex problems for the majority of men and women.

A check mark in the "Yes" column indicates a possible source of your sex problem. More than one "Yes" may mean that your problem is a combination of factors. Review the questions to which you answered "Yes." These are the sources you should read about the most carefully. The information and specific advice for each of your "Yes" answers will be your treatment program.

Solutions for Personal Sources

Personal Source 1 or 2

This information and these suggestions will help you if you checked "Yes" to Personal Source 1 or 2.

General Information

Most of the sources of personal sex problems came from the family conditions in which you grew up. You are the sexual person that you are because of what you learned from this environment. You learned from what your parents told you about sex, your early experiences with sex, and what you observed. The early years of life are very, very important. This is when you learn to be comfortable or not with your body and sexual behavior.

If you come from a family who did not discuss sex much, you are like most people. Even so, parents can still give positive messages about sex. They do this by openly showing affection toward each other and their children. Parents who argue a great deal, rarely hug or kiss, and are not around to comfort and guide give a negative message. From this kind of environment, you learn to be uneasy with showing affection and being close. What you observed your parents doing or not doing in terms of intimacy is crucial.

Some parents give only explicit warnings about sex. In doing so, they sow the seeds of a very negative attitude toward sex. Warnings and cautions about sex are necessary. At the same time, they should be balanced by as many positive statements about sex. All too often they are not. So, a child is left with only the negative ideas. You might have heard warnings and threats of punishment for getting pregnant out of wedlock. You might have learned that sex is dirty or sinful. You might have heard statements about pain or trauma related to sex. All of these can give you a negative view of sexuality.

Sexual abuse is another source of sex problems. The experience with abuse could have been direct or indirect. Either kind can give a person negative ideas about sex. This is very true if the person has not been able to talk with a caring adult about his or her trauma. Such a discussion could have helped place the experience in a healing light.

Also, many men and women grow up with false information and ideas about sex. These can lead to sex problems. For instance, a person might think that sex should always be exciting and amazing. If it has not been, that person may begin to think that something is wrong with him or her. He or she simply does not know that sex varies widely from one time to the next. The person who thinks that he or she is at fault might then take a lot of worry into the next sexual encounter. Doing so causes a problem because he or she focuses on performance, not on pleasure.

All of these things can lead to negative feelings and attitudes about sex. If a person takes these feelings and views into a relationship, they can cause sex problems.

Specific Suggestions

The good news is that there is help for sex problems that come from negative or incorrect sex information. One way to solve personal sex problems is to start with a solid base of correct information. The first six chapters and Appendix A, "Common Sexual Myths," of this Workbook provide that basis.

Personal Source 3, 4, or 5

This information and these suggestions will help you if you checked "Yes" to Personal Source 3, 4, or 5.

General Information

Two things happen to a person who grows up in surroundings that are sexually negative. He or she often is uneasy or anxious about his or her body and about sex. It is best to deal with such feelings as fears. Sadly, most people avoid their fears rather than face them. To conquer a fear, however, a person must face it. The best way to face a fear is to break it down into small, manageable steps and then work through them one step at a time. The longer a person avoids a fear, the harder it is to overcome.

With regard to sex, single people avoid sex by not even dating. A married person may avoid sex in many different ways. The partner might stay up later than the other one, work long hours, or start an argument at the wrong time. A partner might also turn off the television or switch channels when something sexy comes on. Whatever way the person uses to avoid sex, it does not solve the sex problem. In the long run, it is destructive. To add to this problem, partners sometimes do not communicate well. When these happen, the partnership becomes very stressed and unhappy.

Specific Suggestions

The source of your sex problem can be many things. It might come from past sexual abuse. It might come from an experience with sex that made you feel ashamed or embarrassed. It might come from a general fear of sex partners, that is, all men or all women. If your problem comes from one of these sources, you are likely avoiding sex. You must recognize your avoidance and begin to approach sex very slowly. If you are married or have a steady partner, then you have to open up. In this way, you can create conditions that allow you to approach sex and closeness step by step. To do this, you and your partner must agree to the following conditions:

■ Practice sex and being intimate on a regular basis. At the least, this practice should occur twice a week for about 2 hours each time. Most of the time, practicing more often will lead to success more quickly.

- Set aside the time and place for practice so that you have privacy and are not pressured or rushed in any way. Turn off telephones and make sure nothing else will intrude.

- Agree with your partner that the goal is comfort, *not* wild sex. The goal is *not* orgasm, erection, or intercourse.

- Start with behaviors with which you are comfortable, such as hugging or back rubs. Try to include more intimate behaviors each time you practice.

- You may include any behaviors that you and your partner agree on. Also agree that you may stop with anything that causes "too much anxiety." You are the judge of what is "too much anxiety," but try to push yourself each time and do not give up early.

If you agree to these five things, you should notice changes within a couple of weeks. You will begin to have less fear and discomfort with sex and to enjoy sex more. Keep practicing. Do so until you are at ease with all the sexual behaviors that you and your partner want in your relations.

If you are single and have fears of sex, it is important for you to socialize. Put yourself in situations where you can meet potential partners. Remember, you are in control of the situation. Date only people you are at ease with and who seem at ease with their own sexuality. Do not date someone who is insecure. Do not date someone who is rigid in his or her views or sees the world in terms of right and wrong. Do not date someone who puts too much emphasis on sex. Such a person will not help you overcome your problem. Avoid such people. Date only people with whom you feel comfortable.

You might be uncomfortable with seeing or touching your own body. If so, approach the problem by reducing the fear. Again, break down the fear into small, manageable steps, and practice, practice, practice. For instance, start by looking briefly in the mirror at your body while you are dressed in only your underwear. Increase the amount of time you spend looking at your body. A little at a time, expose or touch the part or parts of your body that disturb you the most. In time, you will increase your level of comfort with it. Make sure your practice sessions are frequent and private. Practice several times a week and turn off telephones and lock the doors.

Some people have found that looking at erotic pictures or movies helps reduce fear. It is important, however, that you choose material that does not offend you. The material you choose should be acceptable and not upsetting to you.

Personal Source 6

This information and these suggestions will help you if you checked "Yes" to Personal Source 6.

General Information

If your sex problem is a result of other personal problems, then you must treat those problems first. Review your past. Ask yourself if you had sex problems when you were not feeling depressed, insecure, or worried in any way. If you had no sex problems during better times in the past, then your problem may not be sexual.

Specific Suggestions

Pinpoint the source of the personal problem that is affecting you. The problem might be one that will not pass in time or that you cannot solve yourself. If so, discuss this with your therapist. You and your therapist might agree to refocus your therapy or to refer you for other help. It is not likely that you can make progress to solve a sex problem while you are having other personal problems.

Personal Source 7

This information and these suggestions will help you if you checked "Yes" to Personal Source 7.

General Information

Some people think they have a sex problem when, in fact, they do not. Their problem is either not making quality time for sex or trying to have sex at the "wrong" time. The wrong time is a combination of two things. One, there are conditions that interfere with sex. Two, the environment is not favorable for sex. A couple might be busy with two jobs and have work hours that conflict. They might also be busy with children or parents. Such couples often try to have sex at the wrong time. These couples may try to have sex when they have the opportunity but not the desire. Most of the time, the result is less than satisfying.

Specific Suggestions

First, ask yourself, "What are my priorities?" You may have obligations to work, to children, or to parents. You also have an obligation to your partnership. Often couples put everything else first and do not set aside time for each other. So, sex happens "catch-as-catch-can," not as the natural result of close, intimate time spent together. Sit down with your partner and make plans together. The plans might simply be taking a walk together or having a quiet talk together. You should make plans for short time together every week. You should also make plans for longer times together that may involve a full day, weekend, or vacation. Two things happen when you make plans for being together. One, the times together become a priority. Two, everything else becomes less important, unless there is a crisis.

A second part of this solution is to make an agreement with your partner. Agree that sex can mean a whole range of activities. It does not always have to mean intercourse or result in orgasm. Even if you have the opportunity, you might not feel a desire for sex. If so, agree that either of you can suggest a more limited kind of sex without fear or anger. For example, you may say, "I really feel tired tonight, let's just snuggle for a while." Either you or your partner should accept this option without feeling hurt or rejected.

Personal Source 8

This information and these suggestions will help you if you checked "Yes" to Personal Source 8.

General Information

You may be attracted to members of your own gender and to members of the opposite gender. This is often confusing. Most people think that attractions must be one way or another. If you are wondering about your own sexual direction, you must find out how strong your attractions are. Sex works best when you are having sex with a partner who sexually attracts you. You should not have sex with someone who does not attract you. People do this just because they think it is what is expected or accepted. Such a person will likely have problems. This is especially true in a long-term partnership.

Specific Suggestions

Perhaps your desires for the opposite gender are not strong, but your sex partner is of the opposite gender. If so, then sex problems can occur. This is often the case because sexual direction is very, very hard to change. Accept your sexual direction and seek partners who meet your strongest desires. This is the most rewarding path for most people. This is a very difficult issue. A therapist who has experience in dealing with these issues can often help.

We have dealt with heterosexual couples in which one partner is attracted to those of the same gender. This type of relationship does not always lead to sex problems if the partner also has desire for his or her opposite-gender partner. This also applies to same-gender couples in which one partner has desires for those of the opposite gender. In either type of relationship, the issue is the same—faithfulness and trust. Both types of relationships are open to outside affairs. This issue has more to do with personal morals and choice than with sexual direction.

When one partner has same-gender desires, the couple must discuss the issue of faithfulness. From this talk, they should understand how each is vulnerable and assure each other of faithfulness. Often, such a talk can clear up any misunderstandings, which can lead to anger and withdrawal. So, it is crucial for you to talk openly about being attracted to others and about being faithful.

Solutions for Interpersonal Sources

Interpersonal Source 1 or 2

This information and these suggestions will help you if you checked "Yes" to Interpersonal Source 1 or 2.

General Information

From Chapter 2, you learned that people commonly blame themselves for a sex problem. They do this even when their partner brought the sex problem into the relationship. In a long-term partnership, finding the original source of the problem can sometimes be hard. Try to recall other relationships that were enjoyable and free of stress. If you can, then your partner might have brought the problem into your relationship. If you get along well with your partner and you enjoy sex, then the sex problem is most likely your partner's problem.

Specific Suggestions

If your partner brought the problem, then it is crucial to think of the problem as a couples problem. It is important not to blame your partner. Blaming your partner will only be destructive.

First, discuss the facts with your partner and reassure your partner of your love and attraction. If your talk goes smoothly, you and your partner should be able to agree to work together on the problem.

Second, encourage your partner to pinpoint the source of his or her problem. Then follow the solutions outlined before. Support and help your partner with all the necessary steps so that both of you benefit.

Interpersonal Source 3

This information and these suggestions will help you if you checked "Yes" to Interpersonal Source 3.

General Information

When partners do not communicate, sex problems can occur. This is so because one or both partners become angry or do not understand what is going on with the other. Not talking can also keep a sex problem going even when the problem was caused by something else. This is so because a couple may avoid looking for solutions. Talking about sex is hard, even for couples who communicate well. It is a common issue for most couples who are trying to solve a sex problem.

Specific Suggestions

If you and your partner have this problem, both of you should reread the part about communicating in Chapter 8. Pay very close attention to sender and receiver skills.

Then agree on regular times to meet when you both can practice good communication. Make sure telephone calls and children will not bother you. Schedule meetings at least two or three times a week. Meeting this often will increase the chances of improving your skills.

The third step is to meet with your partner. Each meeting should be from 2 hours to 1 hour long. In the first meeting, talk about the sender and receiver skills that each of you needs to develop. Pinpoint skills that you need to improve for yourself. Do not judge your partner's communication problems.

The fourth step is to talk about affection and sexual intimacy. A good rule is to let your partner know what he or she is doing that you like. Also discuss the types of affection and sex behaviors you want as part of your partnership.

The fifth step is for both you and your partner to keep in mind that there are no right or wrong sexual behaviors. There are only likes and dislikes. One partner may not like a certain behavior or an approach to sex. The other partner may greatly desire it. Being a good lover does not mean knowing some great secret to wonderful sex. Being a good lover means paying attention to your partner's words and actions to learn what your partner does and does not like.

Interpersonal Source 4

This information and these suggestions will help you if you checked "Yes" to Interpersonal Source 4.

General Information

Anger and tension related to your partner will surely get in the way of sexual closeness. For most people, it is impossible to feel like having sex with their partners if they are angry with them. The important question is whether or not your anger is so great or has lasted so long that you cannot put it aside. For some couples in treatment, the anger is so great that progress is not likely.

Specific Suggestions

If you feel anger or tension toward your partner, the first step is to ask yourself a question. Can you put aside your feelings long enough to work on increasing intimacy? If your honest answer is no, no matter how hard you try, then you should seek help. You will need to do one of two things. You can work past your feelings or you can end the relationship. If you believe that your anger or tension can be treated, then go to the second step.

The second step is to try to resolve anger through talking and trying to agree on things. Most couples will find that two things can help solve the problem. First, follow the communication steps in Chapter 8. Second, focus on the causes of anger. Even if you do these two things, you might argue even more, and the tension and anger might get worse. If so, then you may need an outside counselor to help you. Once anger is resolved, you can proceed to work on other sources of your sex problem.

Interpersonal Source 5

This information and these suggestions will help you if you checked "Yes" to Interpersonal Source 5.

General Information

This problem occurs when a person's partner just does not make the person feel sexually aroused. This can be very frustrating. This can happen even when a person has very strong good feelings for a partner and sees many good things in him or her. For some couples, it has always been this way. For other couples, it develops over years of partnership. A person may have sexual desires but just does not find his or her partner arousing. The partner may, in fact, be a very attractive person. On the other hand, the partner might have become less attractive because of weight gain or other changes that come with time.

Specific Suggestions

Perhaps the lack of sexual attraction has always been there. Your partner meets most of your criteria. He or she is a kind, good person; good provider; good parent; humorous; and liked by family. However, your partner may remind you of someone, such as your mother, that you cannot think of in a sexual way. Perhaps, you view your partner as so virtuous or good that it is hard to think of him or her in a sexual way. For example, you might think, "Only a whore could be sexual. My wife, who is the mother of my children, cannot be sexual."

To solve this problem, a couple may need to try to spend time in more erotic and romantic settings. Getting away to a motel or resort for a romantic weekend once in a while can help. A couple might try setting aside time to date each other on a weekly basis. For this, one partner chooses the type of date one time, and the other partner chooses the next time.

There is another possible way to solve the problem. This is the use of erotic materials, such as movies or clothes. You must do this with care and caution. Make sure that the material does not offend either of you. Wearing something sexy or acting in a sexy way may help you see one another in a new light. This can work only if both of you agree to try it and if neither of you is insecure or defensive about it. Attempts at change should be repeated a number of times and not given up after only one.

The lack of sexual desire for one's partner may also have another cause. It could be a result of changes that have occurred over time. Desire in a long-term relationship can be lost in a number of ways.

Always being available for sex and never saying no: Being available all of the time almost always takes away desire for both partners. It is very normal and natural not to always be interested in sex. The person who is willing to have sex all of the time is likely having sex at less than desirable times. Also, with such a partner, the mystery, novelty, and risk of sex are taken away. These are very important for keeping desire alive. The person who is always available is, in effect, saying, "Your appearance or sexual skills do not matter; I'll do it anyway."

Letting your appearance go by not taking care of yourself: If a person does not try to keep himself or herself attractive, he or she is saying, "I don't have to work on this relationship anymore; you'll always be there anyway." On the other hand, keeping yourself attractive says, "I want to look my best for you because you are special."

Being too close and too familiar: Some couples boast that they do everything together. There are few interests, activities, or friends that they do not share. This kind of relationship sounds good on the surface, but it is not good in a long-term relationship. The best long-term partnerships have a good core of interests, activities, and friends that are shared. They also have some interests, activities, and friends that are not shared. Things that are not shared, in fact, add to the relationship and help to decrease too much familiarity. Being too familiar can take away sexual desire. For example, do not always walk around naked in front of your partner, and keep bathroom behaviors private. This has nothing to do with modesty. It has everything to do with keeping mystery in your partnership. Mystery adds to and keeps up desire.

Interpersonal Source 6

This information and these suggestions will help you if you checked "Yes" Interpersonal Source 6.

General Information

Physical attractions to other people are a normal and natural part of life. It is not realistic to expect that they will stop once you are in a relationship. Physical attraction to a person other than your partner does not have to cause a problem. It causes a problem only if you become distracted with the attraction or if you act on it. Being attracted to someone else will not of itself interfere with you and your partner. It can, though, when you already have doubts about your relationship with your partner.

Specific Suggestions

It is much easier to deal with an attraction to someone else when you have not yet acted on it. Once you have acted on it, then you have exposed yourself to a number of risks. These risks include disease, pregnancy, break up of your relationship, and hurting loved ones. They can even include revenge from your partner or the other person's partner. If you have not acted on your attraction but it is hard to stay faithful to your partner, then seek help right away. Share your secrets with a therapist or a trusted friend. Doing so can help you to put the attraction into perspective. You must find out if your "other attraction" is a sign of not being happy with yourself or with your partner. Most of the time, you cannot determine the cause alone. You need the objective point of view of another trusted person.

Solutions for Medical Sources

Medical Source 1

This information and these suggestions will help you if you checked "Yes" to Medical Source 1.

General Information

The use of alcohol or other drugs to excess can have a negative effect on sex in both men and women. Alcohol or other drugs can affect being able to have sex while you are intoxicated or "high." In some cases, the damage can be permanent even after you stop drinking or taking drugs. The treatment of your sex problem can never work as long as you are still abusing alcohol or other drugs. The tolerance level differs from person to person. You might wonder if your use is excessive. Ask yourself and ask a trusted friend if the alcohol or other drugs are in any way causing you problems. Is the alcohol or drug getting in the way of your job or your relationship? Is it causing you problems with money or being productive? Is it keeping you from fulfilling any of your obligations? If the answer is yes, then you have a problem no matter how much or how little you are drinking or taking drugs. Get help for your substance abuse. Then deal with your sex problem.

Specific Suggestions

You might not be sure if alcohol or other drugs are affecting your sex life. If so, you can test yourself. Stop drinking or taking other drugs for one month and see how your sex life is affected. Do not judge your sexual success or failure on the basis of just one encounter. Rather, look at your total record for a month. If you think that a month does not give a full picture, then try sex without alcohol or other drugs for 2 or 3 months. If you cannot stop substance abuse for at least a month, then most likely you do have a problem. For most men and women, one or two drinks do not interfere with sex. The more you drink, however, the more likely alcohol will interfere with sex. How prescribed drugs, street drugs, and over-the-counter drugs affect sex cannot be known for certain.

Medical Source 2

This information and these suggestions will help you if you checked "Yes" to Medical Source 2.

General Information

You should never change or stop taking a prescribed drug without first talking to your doctor. In most cases, your doctor may be able to change your medicine without the change affecting your health. You may think that your sex problem began after you started taking a certain drug. If so, then talking to your doctor is certainly worthwhile.

Specific Suggestions

You and your doctor might have agreed either to stop or change your medication. If so, ask your doctor how long the old medication stays in your system and how long the new one takes to take effect. Do not expect any change until the old medication is out of your system. You should not conclude anything until you have had sex several times over a period of at least 1 month. You cannot conclude anything after having sex only one or two times.

After your doctor has changed your prescription and you have had sex a number of times, you might still be having problems. If so, then the medication may not be the problem. At this point, you should talk to your doctor again or conclude that the sex problem may be a result of other factors. Review the questions in Worksheet 10.1 to see if there are any other possible sources for your problem.

Medical Source 3

This information and these suggestions will help you if you checked "Yes" to Medical Source 3.

General Information

Most of the time with spinal cord injury, not being able to have sex occurs right away. If this is the case, it is clear that the injury has caused the problem. With certain diseases, not being able to have sex comes on slowly over a long period of time. These include heart disease, such as stroke and heart attack, and diabetes. They also include diseases that affect the nerves, such as multiple sclerosis. Men may notice that their erections are less firm or that orgasms are less intense. Women may notice a decrease in vaginal wetness and a decrease in the number of orgasms (see Suggested Readings for more information).

Specific Suggestions

If you have one of these diseases, it is quite likely having an effect on your sex life. However, these diseases by no means condemn you to a life without sex. At worst, you may need to adjust your approach to sex. In most cases, medical and psychological assistance can help you find a sex life that you can enjoy (Wincze & Carey, 1991). It is crucial to follow your doctor's advice to keep your illness under control as much as possible. In many cases, controlling the disease can bring back your ability to have sex.

The next step is to make sure that conditions for sex are favorable for the most part. Also make sure that both you and your partner can accept a sex life that does not exactly match what you enjoyed in the past. Because of your disease, you may be more open to factors that may interfere with sex. For example, noises or fatigue might interfere with sex now, when they did not before. The best approach is for you and your partner to accept the changes in sexual functioning. This means to take the attitude "whatever happens, happens." This approach means you must enjoy each encounter for what it is and not compare it to past ones.

Some people may choose to use a medical method to help them perform better. For men, these include a number of options that range from prescribed drugs to surgical implants. You should discuss the good and bad points of each option with a doctor or therapist who has knowledge of them. There are fewer medical options for women. A decrease in vaginal wetness and orgasm may have a medical cause. One is menopause, and the other is a disease. A doctor can best advise a woman on the use of lubricants or other methods.

Medical Source 4

This information and these suggestions will help you if you checked "Yes" to Medical Source 4.

General Information

In Chapter 4, we discussed medical factors that can have a direct or an indirect effect on sex. They affect sex only because they make sex less appealing or less comfortable. Most of the time, there are many ways to make sex more enjoyable. It is crucial to seek out solutions rather than to withdraw and avoid sex. You can try having sex less often. You can try having sex under certain conditions. You might change the types of sexual behaviors you enjoy. All of these ways are far better than stopping sex entirely.

Specific Suggestions

If a medical condition is having an indirect effect on your sex life, you should find out about the condition. You can find this information through reading or through local support groups. For many of these conditions, there is reading material that can help you adjust to your disease. The latest readings will discuss sex and give some advice and tips (see Suggested Readings for more information).

The first step is to wait until your medical condition is stable and not likely to get worse. During this time, you and your partner must show physical affection toward each other. This is a way to be intimate and does not have to lead to sex. Affection can keep you from being isolated. It also creates the conditions for sex at a later time, when you and your partner are ready.

Local self-help groups are a great source of information. Talking to people with similar problems can help you find ways to make sex better. These self-help groups include people who have had stroke, prostate cancer, back pain, or other diseases. These people are very open and willing to share what they have gone through to help you make your sex life better. Most local newspapers list meeting times and places. These groups welcome new members and their partners.

Medical Source 5

This information and these suggestions will help you if you checked "Yes" to Medical Source 5.

General Information

Medical Source 5 is a crucial for men trying to find the cause of their sex problem. Men normally have erections at night while they are sleeping. These nighttime erections are referred to as *nocturnal penile tumescence* (NPT). It is normal for men to have such erections throughout their lives. Most of the time, a man has from one to six erections while he is sleeping. A man is aware of the erection only if he happens to wake when it is occurring. Most of the time, the erection cycle occurs while a man is dreaming, but the dream does not have to be sexual. Most men think that a full bladder causes nighttime erections, but a full bladder has nothing to do with causing the erection. They are caused by a release of chemicals in the brain that occurs during dreaming. The nighttime or sleeping erection is important. If a man has them, then the cause of the erection problem is likely not a medical one.

Specific Suggestions

Men who have very restless or disturbed sleep may not have sleep erections. The only certain way to know if sleep erections occur is to consult a doctor. Most of the time, this will be a urologist, who is a specialist in sex problems. One instrument used by urologists is a rigiscan, which can be used in the home. The device is worn at night and records all changes in erections. From the printout, the doctor can tell whether or not erections are occurring. Keep this in mind if you have good erections when you view sexy material or masturbate. Your sex problem is not a medical one.

Summary

To this point, you have worked on solutions to the causes of your sex problem. Now, you are ready to master your problem by following the treatments for your specific type of problem. Some problems may respond to more than one of the strategies discussed next. These strategies are useful only after you have done all of the other steps discussed in this Workbook. These treatments will work only if the person has done all of the prior groundwork for mastering sex problems.

Treatment for Specific Problems

Treatment for Erection Problems in Men and for Sexual Arousal Problems in Women

In earlier exercises, you set an ideal time to be with your partner. You made sure that it is a private time without any kinds of distractions. You also began to talk more openly with your partner about matters that are hard to discuss. These exercises were needed to lay the groundwork for this treatment. The aim of this treatment is to increase comfort with physical intimacy. In addition, it will help you to communicate your sexual needs.

Sensate Focus

This treatment is called *sensate focus,* or pleasuring. You and your partner will find ways to be physically intimate that do not include intercourse. This treatment helps regardless of the source of your sex problem. The idea is to give pleasure to each other but not expect or demand intercourse. The following steps will help guide you through this treatment. Keep working on this treatment weekly until you and your partner are at ease with pleasuring.

- Set up one to three times a week that you and your partner can practice sexual touching. This should be a time that you both agree on and a time when you do not feel rushed or tired.

- You and your partner must agree that intercourse will not be a part of the exercise—no matter how aroused you become. You must agree to this for two reasons. One, it takes away the pressure to perform. Second, it allows you to be more flexible and to explore more.

- You should also agree that becoming sexually aroused is not the goal. The goal is simply to enjoy the sensations. If arousal does occur, that is okay, but it is not the goal.

- Through your talks, you should know the activities that are comfortable and that give you pleasure. Are you at ease with genital stimulation or only with holding hands? You should know the comfort level so you do not go beyond that level when you start pleasuring. Each time you have a pleasuring session, you should try to add more activities beyond what you did before.

- Take turns pleasuring each other or pleasure each other at the same time. Try both approaches.

- Practice with as little clothing on as possible. Again, start with your comfort level.

- A pleasuring session should last about 15–30 minutes.

- For some couples, the pleasuring sessions are the most effective when they are very strictly structured. For this, you plan exactly what you will do, when you will do it, and for how long you will do it. Other couples like to take a more open-ended approach and just see what happens. We strongly suggest this open-ended style. However, if progress stalls or stops, a more structured approach is needed.

- Once you have completed a pleasuring session, discuss with your partner what you liked. Try to keep out any negative criticism.

- Keep doing the sessions until you and your partner feel at ease with every kind of pleasuring that both of you want. Do not feel that you have to enjoy all types of pleasuring. If both you and your partner are against certain sexual behaviors, do not include them.

- When you are completely at ease with pleasuring, include intercourse some of the time. Do not feel that you have to include intercourse every time. A good sexual relationship means you are at ease in saying what you want or do not want. It also means you can stop at any time you want without negative reactions or feelings.

This treatment is helpful for single people as well. You must find a partner who is at ease with and accepts the general principles. Avoid partners who think intercourse is the only true sex. Also avoid those who feel that once you start something, you have to finish it with intercourse.

Treatment for Men With Quick Ejaculation

A man and his partner must be realistic about how long a man lasts before he ejaculates. A man must enjoy what he is doing during sex rather than worry about control. One way to treat this problem is for the man to go on with intercourse as long as he can after ejaculating. Many men make the mistake of stopping intercourse and withdrawing as soon as they ejaculate. They also express anger and feelings of failure as soon as they ejaculate. Sudden withdrawal surely takes away the pleasure for a man and his partner. Many men can keep thrusting for many minutes after they ejaculate. By doing so, a man can extend the pleasure for his partner. He also takes away the worry about control for himself. We have found that once a man no longer worries about control, he enjoys sex more and may even last longer.

Another strategy for the man and his partner is to agree on orgasms. Agree that it does not matter if they occur together or if one follows the other. Also agree that it does not matter if one or both of you do not have an orgasm on any one occasion. By agreeing to these things, you get rid of the pressure of trying to control ejaculation. Such an agreement will also likely result in more pleasure for both partners.

For some, neither of these strategies will work. They will not work for a man who ejaculates before entering his partner. They also will not work if the man must wear a condom to prevent disease or pregnancy. In these cases, he may wish to try the "squeeze" technique. With this, the man squeezes the ridge of his penis with two fingers and his thumb below the head of the penis. The squeeze should be firm and last for about 10 seconds. A man should use this when he feels he will ejaculate if sexual stimulation goes on. Most of the time, the squeeze allows a man to last longer when stimulation is resumed. The man may use it before entering his partner or may withdraw and then use it. The squeeze may be applied once or many times during a single sexual encounter.

Treatment for Men and Women Who Have Difficulty Achieving Orgasm

A problem in having an orgasm is often caused by not being aroused enough. Couples may want to use things that cause arousal, such as sexy underwear and fantasies. Even forbidden fantasies can be helpful at times. Other ways to help arousal are new behaviors, new positions, and sex toys. The guideline is to find conditions that are the most arousing and that you and your partner can accept. Most couples who are willing to try new types of stimulation will enjoy more arousal. At no time should you or your partner try something that offends either one. The idea is to arouse you, not to turn you off.

Treatment for Women Who Have Difficulty With Penetration

Women who have a problem with penetration must approach the problem slowly. They must also keep the solution within their control. The basic strategy is to practice penetration a little at a time. Most women prefer to start this treatment alone. You should practice for about 15–30 minutes several times a week. Start penetration at a level that is easy for you. Then increase it a little at a time in each session. You may wish to begin with just looking at your genitals with a hand-held mirror. A next step may be touching the lips of the vagina for a few seconds. To penetrate the vagina, use the middle finger. Increase the time and depth a little at a time until you can insert your finger full length for a couple of minutes. You might wish to practice this while showering or sitting on the bed. You should use whatever setting and position give the most comfort.

After you have practiced alone, you may then want to include your partner. Your partner should also be guided by your comfort level. Increase length of time and depth of penetration a little at a time until full intercourse occurs. Doing this exercise may be a real challenge for a male partner. However, most of the time it works out well if you discuss all the guidelines and what to expect ahead of time.

Treatment for Men and Women Who Have Low Interest or Desire for Sex

Depression or poor partner relations can cause low desire for sex. If neither of these is the case, then a person with low desire may need more stimulation. Sexy movies or magazines can boost desire. For most people, a sexy movie can increase interest in sex for at least 48 hours after the movie. Couples who try to make sex romantic or who go away on vacation increase interest in sex. This interest can last for several weeks or longer. Of course, going on a vacation solely to boost your sex life may be expensive. However, it is important to try to boost your sex life once in a while by any of these ways.

Summary

This chapter has focused on exercises and treatments to help you master your sex problem. So, there is no exercise at the end of this chapter. Most of the strategies in this chapter have to be practiced more than once to produce results. Keep talking with your partner to assess your progress.

Chapter 10 Review

Answer by circling **T** (True) or **F** (False). Answers are provided in Appendix B.

1. The goal of therapy is to restore sex to what it was
   before you had problems.   **T   F**

2. Sex always has to be planned carefully to be enjoyed.   **T   F**

3. A single person should look for the most attractive person
   for help in overcoming a sex problem.   **T   F**

4. The first step in solving a sex problem is to gather
   accurate information.   **T   F**

5. Blaming your partner for the sex problem will get in
   the way of therapy.   **T   F**

Worksheet 10.1. Common Causes or Sources of Sex Problems

Personal Sources:

1. When you were a child or teenager, did messages about sex or your body make you upset or uneasy? ☐ Yes ☐ No

2. As a child or teenager, did you receive information about sex? Do you get incorrect information about sex? ☐ Yes ☐ No

3. As a child or teenager, were you a victim of sexual abuse? Did you know of friends or family who were? ☐ Yes ☐ No

4. As an adult, have you ever had an experience with sex that made you feel upset or ashamed? ☐ Yes ☐ No

5. Do you have general anger toward or fear of the opposite sex? ☐ Yes ☐ No

6. Do you now have a personal problem that is not related to sex? This might be low self-esteem, worry, depression, trauma, or fear. ☐ Yes ☐ No

7. When you have an opportunity for sex, is it in a private, comfortable place? ☐ Yes ☐ No

8. Do you feel confused about your sexual direction? ☐ Yes ☐ No

Interpersonal Sources:

1. Is your sex partner tense or uneasy about sex or does he or she seem uninterested? ☐ Yes ☐ No

2. Does your partner have his or her own sex problems? ☐ Yes ☐ No

3. Is it hard for you to talk with your sex partner? ☐ Yes ☐ No

4. Do you feel tension or anger toward your sex partner? ☐ Yes ☐ No

5. Do you lack physical attraction toward your partner? ☐ Yes ☐ No

6. Do you have a strong physical attraction toward someone other than your partner? ☐ Yes ☐ No

Medical Sources:

1. Are you now using or abusing alcohol or other drugs? ☐ Yes ☐ No

2. Are you taking a drug to treat a mental problem, high blood pressure, ulcers, or seizures? ☐ Yes ☐ No

3. Do you have diabetes, heart disease, nerve disease, or spinal cord injury? ☐ Yes ☐ No

4. Do you have a health condition that causes you to feel self-conscious or embarrassed? Do you have one that causes pain, fatigue, or nausea? ☐ Yes ☐ No

5. If you are male, do you *not* have erections at any time? That is, when you are with a partner, when you masturbate, or at night when you wake up? ☐ Yes ☐ No

Worksheet 10.1. Common Causes or Sources of Sex Problems

Personal Sources:

1. When you were a child or teenager, did messages about
   sex or your body make you upset or uneasy?   ☐ Yes ☐ No

2. As a child or teenager, did you receive information about
   sex? Do you get incorrect information about sex?   ☐ Yes ☐ No

3. As a child or teenager, were you a victim of sexual abuse?
   Did you know of friends or family who were?   ☐ Yes ☐ No

4. As an adult, have you ever had an experience with sex
   that made you feel upset or ashamed?   ☐ Yes ☐ No

5. Do you have general anger toward or fear of the
   opposite sex?   ☐ Yes ☐ No

6. Do you now have a personal problem that is not related
   to sex? This might be low self-esteem, worry, depression,
   trauma, or fear.   ☐ Yes ☐ No

7. When you have an opportunity for sex, is it in a private,
   comfortable place?   ☐ Yes ☐ No

8. Do you feel confused about your sexual direction?   ☐ Yes ☐ No

Interpersonal Sources:

1. Is your sex partner tense or uneasy about sex or does he
   or she seem uninterested?   ☐ Yes ☐ No

2. Does your partner have his or her own sex problems?   ☐ Yes ☐ No

3. Is it hard for you to talk with your sex partner?   ☐ Yes ☐ No

4. Do you feel tension or anger toward your sex partner?   ☐ Yes ☐ No

5. Do you lack physical attraction toward your partner?   ☐ Yes ☐ No

6. Do you have a strong physical attraction toward someone
   other than your partner?   ☐ Yes ☐ No

Medical Sources:

1. Are you now using or abusing alcohol or other drugs? ☐ Yes ☐ No

2. Are you taking a drug to treat a mental problem, high blood pressure, ulcers, or seizures? ☐ Yes ☐ No

3. Do you have diabetes, heart disease, nerve disease, or spinal cord injury? ☐ Yes ☐ No

4. Do you have a health condition that causes you to feel self-conscious or embarrassed? Do you have one that causes pain, fatigue, or nausea? ☐ Yes ☐ No

5. If you are male, do you *not* have erections at any time? That is, when you are with a partner, when you masturbate, or at night when you wake up? ☐ Yes ☐ No

Chapter 11

Continuing Progress and Preventing Relapse

Off to a Good Start

If you have read this Workbook to this point, then you are off to a good start. You are off to an even better start if your partner has also read this material. If you have done each exercise, then you will have set your goals and treatments for mastering your problem. Also, you and your partner have achieved some goals and worked together on other goals. A very important part of your work has been in setting certain times for practice that you can count on. The times and places for practice should ensure that there is as little stress and distraction as possible. Whether you practice alone or with a partner, the conditions must be private and free of stress.

In spite of your best efforts and your best intentions, working on your sex problem may be hard. It may seem like work and may also be upsetting at times. If you are working with a partner, you and your partner may become upset with each other. Working directly on your sex problem may bring up past, unpleasant memories. These memories might discourage and even keep you from facing your problem. Such feelings are not unusual. You can overcome these feelings if you are able to pinpoint what is happening to you and why.

What To Do if You Start To Avoid Practice

For a while, you might not notice that you are avoiding your problem. At first, the reasons for not practicing may seem reasonable. "I'm really busy at work." "I'm having guests stay with me in my house." "I'm having my period" or "My partner is having her period." "I've had a cold." If you are working with a partner to master your problem, it is common for both of you to make up excuses. After all, it may be very hard and emotionally draining to face your sex problem.

If you have not practiced for a period of one week, you should carefully review the reasons. Perhaps you did not place much importance on practice and so put other things ahead of sex practice. Would you have picked up a winning lottery prize at the time you had planned to practice? If your answer is yes, then most likely you are avoiding practice. If your answer is no, then not being able to practice most likely reflects real problems, not avoidance. Make a commitment to practice next week.

If you think that either you or your partner is avoiding sex practice, then you must pinpoint the reasons. The most common reason is a lack of confidence or trust in how your partner is going to respond. This is especially true if there has been a lot of anger and blaming related to sex problems in the past. In order to practice, you have to be reassured that it is okay to make mistakes. You also have to be sure that you will not be criticized by your partner. Avoidance is common in couples who have never discussed sex much and have a lot of anger toward each other.

If there is avoidance, you can take a number of steps:

- **Commitment:** Mention that you are concerned that you have not been able to practice consistently. Ask your partner to join you in making a better plan to stick to practice. Steer away from blame. Make sure that practice is convenient for both of you and that both of you are committed.

- **Comfort:** Ask your partner if he or she is comfortable with what was planned. It is crucial that you are not trying to practice something that seems overwhelming. Remember, you can make most types of practice simpler by starting with easier steps. For instance, perhaps you had planned to practice hugging and touching your partner but find these too overwhelming. If so, you can simply talk to each other and hold hands, rather than embracing.

- **Expectations:** Review with your partner the details of practice. Review time, place, length of practice, and frequency of practice. You and your partner might differ in what you expect from practice. This can cause problems. Each partner may be waiting for the other to take the first steps and to make specific plans. Be sure that after your discussion, you both understand and agree on all of the details.

- **Goals:** Review your goals. What changes do you expect to achieve and how much time do you expect them to take? If you are working with a partner, are your goals the same? Sometimes people think that progress has been too slow. They become discouraged and so avoid practice. Most of the time, lasting change for most sex problems takes many months of work. However, changes that help to relieve a problem can occur sooner. Just learning about sex problems and how to deal with them helps many people. Much of the time, relief comes from talking with a sex partner when it leads to support rather than to blame. Prepare yourself for some relief of your problem after you read about it and set out a treatment plan.

Reevaluating Goals

Perhaps you have reviewed the four steps of commitment, comfort, expectations, and goals. Perhaps you have renewed your practice. If you still cannot make progress, you may need to review your overall goals. Are they realistic for you? You may need to review the possible sources of your problem in Chapter 10. Have you missed any possible sources? Have you refused to admit certain facts that might be causing the problem? For instance, some couples cannot admit that they are no longer attracted to each other or that they are not in love. Do not confuse other deep feelings for sexual attraction or love. You might feel indebted or obligated. You might really admire or feel very close to your partner. You can have these same good feelings for a brother, sister, or best friend. They do not necessarily lead to sexual feelings. If you are not sure about your sexual attraction to your partner, admit this. Then, you can work on it directly.

Other possibilities may be getting in the way of your progress. If you cannot figure out what they are through this review or talks with your partner, then you may need professional help.

Working With a Therapist

If you are still avoiding practice or if you cannot pinpoint the nature of your problem, then discussion with your therapist may help. If you are not currently seeing a therapist, consider the following. Not all therapists are comfortable working with sex problems. Also, not all therapists have the expertise to do so. To find the best therapist for your problem, you should ask around. You might be embarrassed to ask friends or family. If so, you should ask your family doctor to suggest someone. There might be a university near you. If so, you might call the head of the psychiatry or psychology department. You might call the head of your state's group of psychologists or psychiatrists. You can find these phone numbers in your phone directory.

Once you have the names of some therapists, call them and ask questions over the telephone. Ask how long the therapist has been working with sex problems. Also ask whether or not this is a specialty. Ideally, you want to be able to "connect" with a therapist. You will want one who has experience in treating sex problems and one you feel at ease with.

A therapist is someone to help you if you are stuck and to help keep you on track. For many people, this support is needed to get things going in the right direction.

Your goals may not be realistic or may not fit with those of your partner. If so, a therapist can also help you to set new goals.

Exercise

You must clearly understand what your goals are and how long you are willing to work toward them. Write down your goals and the date when you think you can achieve your goals. Next, write down the things that you think might keep you from achieving your goals. Doing this will help you to pinpoint realistic delays and "excuses."

Chapter 11 Review

Answer by circling **T** (True) or **F** (False). Answers are provided in Appendix B.

1. For most sex problems you can see some change right
   away just from correct information.   T   F

2. A common cause of avoiding practice is the concern that
   your partner will criticize you.   T   F

3. Most sex problems take years of work to correct.   T   F

4. Therapists can be helpful in telling a couple who is to
   blame for the sex problem.   T   F

5. The best way to find a good therapist is through the
   "yellow pages."   T   F

Chapter 12

Maintaining Gains and Preventing Relapse

Reviewing Your Progress From the Start of the Workbook

At this point, you should have had some positive changes in your sex problem. You can evaluate change on a number of levels. The list in Worksheet 12.1 is a review of the important areas in which change should occur. To review the areas and the extent of change and progress, look at Worksheet 12.1. Check off the degree of change you believe you have had for each area.

Worksheet 12.1 should make clear to you that change in a sex problem can occur on many levels. Also, you can work on each level separately. The worksheet lists the chapters in this Workbook that deal with each area. If you checked "No Change," there are a couple of possible reasons. Perhaps you knew the information before you started this Workbook. Perhaps your problem requires more work and time.

If you checked "Much Improvement" or "Some Improvement" for most areas, then you have made good progress. Keeping that progress going and not slipping back are important. You can take some specific steps to make sure that you keep making progress.

Identifying When You Have Slipped Back

You have gained knowledge about sex and understanding of your sex problem. These most likely will not change back to what they were before you began this Workbook. If you do forget some things, a quick review will remind you of the important information. Reread the first few chapters of this Workbook and the common myths about sex in Appendix A. More likely, progress will slip in terms of sexual behaviors. Areas that might change are

- how often you show affection toward a partner,
- how often you have sexual contacts with a partner,
- your comfort level in approaching sex, and
- the quality of your sexual experiences.

For each of these areas, you should set a range of expectations that you can accept. Certainly you can expect your experiences with sex to differ each time. Some may be great and memorable. Others may be mild and even not so good. This difference is normal. How good or how bad any one experience is should not determine if you are having a problem. Instead, it is the overall picture or pattern of your sexual behavior that counts. You have to decide what is, and what is not, an acceptable pattern for you. Some people, for instance, may say that they are having a problem if they are having sex less than once a day. Others may say that less than once every 6 months is a problem. For each of the four areas of change, set an acceptable range that you can measure. Falling below that range will be a signal that you are slipping back.

Here are some examples to help you set what is acceptable and to know when you are having a problem. These are suggestions only. You must decide what is best for you.

- ***Frequency of Affection:*** You might decide that affection should occur at least once a day. Affection may mean saying a kind word or kissing or hugging a partner. Missing a single day without affection should not cause you alarm. Perhaps seven straight days without affection should cause you concern.

- ***Frequency of Sex:*** Decide how often you would like for sex to occur and the point that you should become concerned. Again, just because you fall below this frequency does not mean you should become alarmed. You decide what would be a warning sign for you.

- ***Comfort Level for Sex:*** You can measure comfort level on a scale from 1 to 10. On the scale, 1 means *very, very uncomfortable*; 5 means *comfortable*; 10 means *very, very comfortable*. See the scale below. For instance, you might decide that a comfort level for sex at 3 or less three times in a row calls for a change.

1	2	3	4	5	6	7	8	9	10
Very Uncomfortable				Comfortable				Very Comfortable	

■ *Quality of Sex*: You can also measure quality of sex, as decided by you and your partner, on a scale. See the scale below. Use a similar guideline for deciding when you should become alarmed.

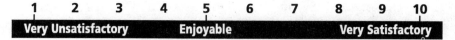

1	2	3	4	5	6	7	8	9	10
Very Unsatisfactory				Enjoyable				Very Satisfactory	

If you fall below the expectations that you have set, then it is time to review what might be causing the problem. Most of the time, a major step is just seeing that there is a problem. You can correct it simply by reviewing the treatment that helped you before. When you set clear expectations that you can measure, you can get back on track before a problem goes on for too long. If you allow a problem to go on for too long, then you may have a hard time in correcting it. If you are working with a partner, it is crucial to set your expectations together. Both of you should agree on what is a cause for alarm in each area. You should also keep track of how you are doing by talking. By doing these things, you can keep from slipping back and you can maintain your gains.

Building Structure To Maintain Gains

Relapses occur either slowly or after some major change in a person's life. When a slip occurs slowly over time, most likely a person has become lazy about his or her sex life. Your sex life needs constant attention for it to stay rewarding and enjoyable. You must always be sensitive to your own mental and physical health. Also, you must always be sensitive to the conditions that are best for you for sex. If you have a steady partner, then you must also be sensitive to the conditions that are best for your partner for sex. Just because you love each other or support and comfort each other does not mean that sex will be great. Sex takes energy and attention. Unless you make an effort, it is likely to be less satisfying than you would like.

Perhaps sex has changed after a major event in your life. If so, you will need to determine what that event has meant to you and why it is affecting your sex life. Some events, such as having a new baby, will almost always affect your sex life. A new baby brings along fatigue, worry, and constant demands on your time. These almost always decrease the frequency and quality of your sex. When sex has changed because of such an event, it is very important to talk to your partner about it. Most likely, you will have to change your expectations for sex while an event is affecting you. Set expectations and a strategy to help you deal with the event while it is affecting you. For instance, in the case of a new baby, you may need to change how often you have sex and the kind of sex you have. Plan to get away with each other once in a while to refresh your sexual experience. You might also agree to touch or fondle each other more but to have intercourse less. All these adjustments help to bridge the time when you are being affected by an event. Remember, sex is not an all-or-nothing event. Instead, it is a whole range of events.

Final Words

The procedures described in this Workbook will work for you if you are motivated for change. Also, you must be persistent and must read and follow the instructions carefully. If you are working with a partner, your partner must be accepting and noncritical for you to succeed. Many people reading this Workbook may not currently have a partner. For them, there are still many helpful suggestions and exercises that can be worked on without a partner. Also, this knowledge can help a single person build a rewarding sex life with a partner in the future.

Congratulations! You have worked very hard to get to this point and you deserve much credit for the work that you have done. We sincerely hope that you are well on your way to improving your sex life.

Exercise

Review all of the check marks in the "No Change" column on Worksheet 12.1. Write out the reasons that you think have had a part in your lack of change. Use these to decide what your next course of action should be. If you are working with a partner, compare your answers and decide together on your next step.

Chapter 12 Review

Answer by circling **T** (True) or **F** (False). Answers are provided in Appendix B.

1. Sexual knowledge that you gain will most likely stay
    with you over time.   **T F**

2. A decrease in your comfort with sex means that you
    are slipping back.   **T F**

3. Frequency of sex is known for each age group, and
    you should try to match it for your age.   **T F**

4. Most people have sex less often after the birth of a child. **T F**

5. Being motivated for change is one of the most important
    factors for making your sex life better.   **T F**

Worksheet 12.1. Areas of Change and Degrees of Improvement

Area of Change

1. General level of information about sex problems (Chapters 1–4)

   ☐ Much Improvement   ☐ Some Improvement   ☐ No Change

2. Detailed information about my own sex problem (Chapters 5–7)

   ☐ Much Improvement   ☐ Some Improvement   ☐ No Change

3. Talking about sex problems with a partner (Chapters 8 & 9)

   ☐ Much Improvement   ☐ Some Improvement   ☐ No Change

4. Knowing exactly what my sex problem is (Chapter 10)

   ☐ Much Improvement   ☐ Some Improvement   ☐ No Change

5. Knowing the sources of my sex problem (Chapter 10)

   ☐ Much Improvement   ☐ Some Improvement   ☐ No Change

6. Knowing how to work on my sex problem (Chapters 10 & 11)

   ☐ Much Improvement   ☐ Some Improvement   ☐ No Change

7. Being able to work in a systematic way on my sex problem (Chapter 10)

   ☐ Much Improvement   ☐ Some Improvement   ☐ No Change

8. Being able to pinpoint when I am avoiding working on my sex problem (Chapter 11)

   ☐ Much Improvement   ☐ Some Improvement   ☐ No Change

9. My attitude toward my sex problem (Entire Workbook)

   ☐ Much Improvement   ☐ Some Improvement   ☐ No Change

10. Mastery of my sex problem (Entire Workbook)

   ☐ Much Improvement   ☐ Some Improvement   ☐ No Change

Worksheet 12.1. Areas of Change and Degrees of Improvement

Area of Change

1. General level of information about sex problems (Chapters 1–4)

   ☐ Much Improvement ☐ Some Improvement ☐ No Change

2. Detailed information about my own sex problem (Chapters 5–7)

   ☐ Much Improvement ☐ Some Improvement ☐ No Change

3. Talking about sex problems with a partner (Chapters 8 & 9)

   ☐ Much Improvement ☐ Some Improvement ☐ No Change

4. Knowing exactly what my sex problem is (Chapter 10)

   ☐ Much Improvement ☐ Some Improvement ☐ No Change

5. Knowing the sources of my sex problem (Chapter 10)

   ☐ Much Improvement ☐ Some Improvement ☐ No Change

6. Knowing how to work on my sex problem (Chapters 10 & 11)

   ☐ Much Improvement ☐ Some Improvement ☐ No Change

7. Being able to work in a systematic way on my sex problem (Chapter 10)

   ☐ Much Improvement ☐ Some Improvement ☐ No Change

8. Being able to pinpoint when I am avoiding working on my sex problem (Chapter 11)

   ☐ Much Improvement ☐ Some Improvement ☐ No Change

9. My attitude toward my sex problem (Entire Workbook)

   ☐ Much Improvement ☐ Some Improvement ☐ No Change

10. Mastery of my sex problem (Entire Workbook)

    ☐ Much Improvement ☐ Some Improvement ☐ No Change

Appendix A

Common Sexual Myths

In our society, it has only recently become okay to talk about sex. So, many people have not had access to correct facts and knowledge about sex. They have learned much of what they know about sex through jokes or through friends who do not know any more than they do. As a result, many people believe the myths they have learned about men and women as sexual beings. Belief in these myths can place a great deal of strain on a sexual relationship. That strain can cause or help maintain a sex problem in one or both partners.

We have described some of the most common sexual myths that we have come across in our therapy program. Some of these beliefs might not apply to you and your partner. Others might. Read over these 13 most common sexual myths. Discuss with your partner those that seem to apply to you and your partner.

Myth 1: "Bigger Is Better"

A very common myth is that a man with larger penis is "more masculine" or more attractive to women. Here are some facts:

Penis length and width vary somewhat when the penis is not aroused. However, most penises become roughly the same size when they are erect. Certainly, there are large ones and there are small ones. Extremes are rare just as people who are shorter than 4 feet or taller than 7 feet are rare. Most men will have erect penises that are between 5 and 7 inches in length.

The crucial point is that size does not matter for sexual enjoyment. First, most of the time, the vagina will adjust to the size of the penis. Second, arousal in a woman occurs at the outer one-third of the vagina, mostly around the clitoris. The penis stretches and rubs the skin around the clitoris and outer vagina. This produces the most pleasure.

Myth 2: "Anywhere, Anytime"

Another myth is that a "real" man should be ready, willing, and able to have sex any time. However, it is the rare man who always wants sex. For instance, a major survey was done by Kinsey, Pomeroy, and Martin, in 1948. They reported on the average number of times a married couple has sex. For people over age 61, it was once per week. For people 16–20 years old, it was four times per week. Many factors can affect the degree of sexual desire that both men and women feel. We discuss some of the more important ones here. Mood states can have a big effect on your desire. When you are feeling happy and relaxed, you are more likely to be aroused. If you feel tired, down, or anxious, have "things on your mind," or are ill, you will feel less like having sex. Also, it is common for men not to be able to get an erection when they are under much stress.

Alcohol is a drug that many people do not understand. Alcohol is a depressant, which means it slows the body down. It also makes a person more relaxed and so makes a person less inhibited. So, when you drink, you may feel more aroused because you are less inhibited. However, a man may also find it harder to get an erection because the body has been slowed down. In fact, many men who have had a lot to drink cannot get an erection while the alcohol is still in the system. Of course, when we say "a lot," this amount differs from person to person. It can be as little as two or three drinks.

Another factor that affects interest in sex is age. It is quite normal for people to want and have sex throughout their lives. In general, the desire for sex and the frequency of sex decrease with increasing age. Another change is common for older men. They may need more time and more direct stimulation of the penis to get an erection and to have an orgasm.

Myth 3: "I Should Be Able To Last All Night"

Another myth is that a man should be able to "last forever" during sex. This myth has been passed on through books, magazines, films, and jokes. In many movies, the young leading man has sex with many women and never seems to ejaculate. So, a lot of normal men think that they ejaculate prematurely because they cannot "go on forever."

Premature ejaculation is a distinct problem and does not just mean that a man ejaculates too quickly. Most of the time, a man will ejaculate more quickly if he has constant stimulation (rubbing). Little is known about how long a man takes to ejaculate. This is because the time it takes to ejaculate differs greatly both among men and for one man from one time to the next. Kinsey et al. (1948) did report that, on average, men take from 30 seconds to 15 minutes to ejaculate during sex.

It is not important how long sex takes. What is important is that you and your partner are at ease and enjoy the experience. There are many ways of enjoying sex (see Myth 7) and many ways it can last and be pleasurable. Enjoyable sex does not depend solely on how long a man takes to ejaculate.

Myth 4: "Too Much Masturbation Is Bad"

Many men and women still believe that masturbating is wrong or even harmful. Most people now know that masturbating will not cause hairy palms or blindness. However, some people do believe that it somehow uses up the "sex drive." Masturbation is normal and is enjoyed by most men and women. Just like sex with a partner, it has no dangerous or bad effects. Sexual desire depends on many factors (Myth 2). Sex drive is not a limited quantity, like fuel in a car, that can be used up. Of course, you may feel slightly less aroused right after masturbating, just as you would after having sex. Also, there is a period of time after orgasm when a man cannot get an erection. This is called the *refractory period*. You can become aroused as soon as this period has ended and you are stimulated.

Myth 5: "Someone With a Sex Partner Does Not Masturbate"

Many people believe that if you have a happy and fulfilling sex life, you should not need to masturbate. A person does not masturbate to fill a physical need but simply to enjoy the pleasure. There are many reasons that people may feel a desire to masturbate. A person who masturbates is in no way strange, oversexed, or immature. It is not a sign that you are disloyal to your partner. Kinsey et al. (1948) found that the average married person over 25 years old masturbates about once every 2 weeks.

Myth 6: "Fantasizing About Something Else Means I'm Not Happy With What I Have"

"If I fantasize about other partners or other types of sex, then it must mean that I don't love my partner." This belief often causes much guilt over something that is very normal—fantasy. Thinking about other people or behaviors, even during sex, can bring a lot of pleasure. It is also very common. Having fantasies is normal and harmless. Some people fantasize many times a day. Some people do not ever fantasize. Keep in mind that just because you imagine something does not mean that you really would do it or would want to do it.

Myth 7: "Women Won't Like Me if I Can't Get It Up"

This myth is similar to Myths 1 and 3. It is that women are not attracted to men who cannot get erections. Some men believe this because they cannot make a woman pregnant without an erection. Others believe this because they cannot give a woman pleasure without an erection.

First, an erection and ejaculation are not the same thing at all. It is ejaculation that causes a woman to get pregnant. A man can ejaculate even if he does not have an erection. Also, if the woman is aroused enough, the penis can enter the vagina, even when it is less than firm.

The second half of the myth is also untrue. It says that a woman cannot be satisfied unless the man has an erection. This myth comes from a fixation on the penis. Sex does not equal intercourse. Sex can be enjoyed in many ways. Penetration of the vagina by the penis is only one way. Kissing, fondling, caressing, and oral sex give much pleasure in themselves. All of these are ways of giving and receiving pleasure and reaching orgasm without intercourse. Sex manuals are a good source of ideas. Using a sex manual is neither wrong nor "dirty" and can be fun. In fact, a man's not getting an erection once in a while is a good reason for a couple to try new things.

Myth 8: "If I Can't Get It Up, I Must Not Really Love My Partner"

At some time in their adult lives, most men will not be able to get or keep an erection. Not being able to get an erection is far more common than most men think, but it is not openly talked about. McCarthy (1988) found that 90% of men will have had an erection failure at least once by the age of 40. Not being able to "get it up" is a common, normal occurrence that can happen for many reasons. It is a problem only when it begins to get in the way of sexual enjoyment. Many men and women believe that when a man cannot get an erection, he does not love his partner. Of course, not caring for or being attracted to your partner can make it more difficult to get an erection. However, not getting an erection does not mean that you do not love your partner. There are many reasons that men may not be able to get or keep an erection. Some are fatigue, depression, stress, illness, drinking to excess, and so on. There are a number of reasons for erection failure that occurs on a regular basis. These are discussed in Chapter 5.

Myth 9: "If a Woman Doesn't Initiate Sex, She's Just Not Interested In Sex"

There are many things that can have an effect on male sexual behavior. There are also many things that can have an effect a woman's sexual desire and behavior.

These factors include stress, fatigue, alcohol in the system, illness, and drug side effects. All of these can have a major effect on a woman's desire for sex. For instance, a woman's partner might have had an erection problem in the past. If so, she might worry about putting pressure on him to perform. She might even avoid hugging, kissing, or holding hands. She thinks that her partner will take these as a signal that he must perform by having intercourse. At the same time, the man might avoid starting any kind of sexual activity. He thinks that his partner does not want any kind of intimacy if she cannot have intercourse. So both partners "lose."

Most likely, both partners would like to be physically intimate in some way again. However, neither wants to start anything because of how he or she thinks the other partner will react. The easiest way to fix this problem is to talk about it! Find out why your partner no longer starts sexual activity and let him or her know how you feel. If one or both of you feel uneasy about putting pressure on you to perform, make a deal. Decide that the two of you will start to be physically close again, but with an understanding. For a certain length of time, no matter how aroused either of you becomes, you will not have intercourse. Stick to this agreement even if you have an erection. In this way, you and your partner can bring back some physical closeness and not feel a pressure to perform.

Myth 10: "If My Partner Doesn't Reach Orgasm, It Means I'm Not Sexually Good Enough"

It is hard for many women to reach an orgasm. Many women enjoy sex and feel fulfilled even though they may never or hardly ever have an orgasm. Over the past 10 years, the media has put pressure on many women and their partners. It has done this by reporting on women who have orgasms more often or have multiple orgasms.

When a woman thinks she should have an orgasm every time or several in a row, she begins to focus on this. She forgets that the point of sex is pleasure. She also forgets that she can enjoy pleasure in many ways, with or without an orgasm. So, she puts pressure on herself to perform a certain way. She shortchanges herself and her partner—just as man who equates sex with having an erection does.

At the same time, many men think that their performance is not good enough if their partners do not have at least one orgasm. So, both partners put pressure on themselves. They think they must perform in a certain way during sex because of what the media has said. If you or your partner has ever fallen into this trap, the best thing to do is talk about it. By talking about your expectations for sex, you can help each other get back on the right track. The right track is to remember that sex is for enjoyment and pleasure. Anything that you do that makes either one of you feel pressured or uneasy is not going to help you reach that goal.

When you do talk, talk about the things that each of you enjoys, such as hugging, kissing, and fantasizing. Tell each other about these things. At the same time, think about the things that make each of you feel pressured to perform. Tell each other about these, too. Talking openly about these issues can help you both figure out what you do and do not enjoy. It is the only way that either of you is going to discover the way the other feels.

Myth 11: "If a Man Knows That He Might Not Be Able to Get or Keep an Erection, It's Unfair for Him To Start Sexual Activity With His Partner"

This widely held belief is not true at all! What is unfair is to assume that you know what your partner thinks without asking her. Many men say they *know* that their partners do not want sex of any kind because they would be too frustrated if they could not "go all the way." Often, the men say they know this, not from something their partners have said, but from the way they act. For instance, these men assume that their partners no longer start any kind of sex because they do not want to have sex. But remember Myth 9. There are many reasons a woman might not want sex. Very often a woman no longer starts sex because she is trying to be considerate. She does not want to put any pressure on her partner to perform. The only way you can find out what your partner thinks is to be direct and ask her.

Many men think that a woman will become too frustrated during sex if she cannot have intercourse. This might be true only if she is used to having an orgasm and becomes very aroused but does not have one. What makes a woman have a climax is stimulation of the clitoris. The clitoris is part of the *external* female genitals. So, it can be stimulated in many ways, manually and by oral sex, to bring a woman to a climax.

Myth 12: "People Who Are in Love Should Automatically Know What Their Partners Desire. Sex Should Be Spontaneous—It Isn't Romantic if You Ask Your Partner What He or She Enjoys"

Every human body is a little bit different. So, each one responds to sexual stimulation in different ways. You may have an area of the body that is very sensitive to sexual touching. That area may not be sensitive at all for other people. Regardless of the number of sex partners you have had in the past, you must talk to your current partner. Unless you have talked to your current partner about it, you cannot know for sure what he or she enjoys. Just because your partner moves or groans in a certain way does not mean he or she is aroused by what you are doing. The only way to know for sure is to ask him or her and listen to what he or she tells you. Likewise, you must tell him or her what you like.

Many people think such talks are not romantic. It is not romantic when two people fumble around during sex, not knowing for sure what the other likes. Once you know about each other's likes and dislikes, you will not need to talk as much during sex. But, you need to give yourselves the chance to find out for certain first.

Myth 13: "Focusing More Intensely on Your Level of Erection— Trying Harder—Is the Best Way To Get an Erection"

Many men who have had problems getting or keeping an erection think that they should focus on their penis during sex. This focus is likely the least effective way to get an erection. What causes an erection in a man are sexy thoughts and behaviors. Focusing on a penis that is not getting erect is certainly not a way to become aroused. So, this kind of "trying" to get or keep an erection is not going to work. More important, you need to remind yourself of the goal of sex. The goal is giving and receiving pleasure with someone you feel close to. Sex should not be work. That is what it often becomes for men whose entire focus is on getting an erection.

Remember, sex does not equal an erection, and it does not equal intercourse. There are many ways for you and your partner to enjoy each other's bodies. Intercourse is only one of them. Be adventurous! Talk to your partner and find new ways that the two of you can enjoy one another!

Appendix B

Answers to Chapter Review Questions

Chapter 2

1. False. It is common for men and women to masturbate their entire lives. This is true even if they are in a loving, sexual relationship with a partner. It is normal for a man or woman to masturbate. It is also normal for a man or woman not to masturbate.

2. False. Many factors can affect a man's erection. How attractive or willing a partner is are not the only factors.

3. True. It is common for both men and women to avoid talking about their sex problem and to avoid sex.

4. False. It is much more common for men than for women to "test out" whether or not sex will work in other situations.

5. False. If you avoid all kinds of physical affection, you will only grow apart more. It will also make the sex problem worse. It is best for a couple to focus on the pleasures of physical affection.

Chapter 3

1. False. What a person learns is the most important influence on how he or she behaves as an adult. This is very true for messages and experiences about sex that a person has as a child.

2. True. Another common term is *sexual orientation*.

3. True. It is common for both men and women to have "forbidden" fantasies about sex.

4. False. Research shows that both men and women masturbate throughout their lives even if they are happily married.

5. False. Many factors can cause a couple to no longer enjoy sex with each other. These include medical and situation factors.

Chapter 4

1. Diabetes, heart disease, and diseases that affect the nerves can all have a *direct* effect on being able to have sex.

2. Back pain, infections, and lung disease can all have an *indirect* effect on being able to have sex.

3. True. Many drugs used to treat depression can decrease a person's desire for sex and being able to have an orgasm.

4. False. No food improves or increases desire for or response to sex. Good health and good nutrition are important for sex.

5. False. No street drug is known to help a person function better sexually.

Chapter 5

1. True. All of these emotions cause an increase in heart rate, breathing rate, and blood pressure.

2. False. Diabetes does interfere with sex for most men. Other factors, such as how aroused a man feels, can override the negative effects. Diabetes is a factor against sex but does not always completely stop a man from being able to have sex.

3. False. A focus on pleasure is always better than a focus on performance.

4. True. The more a person worries about other factors, the more problems a person will have with sex.

5. False. Many factors can take away pleasure from sex in spite of an available, willing partner. Your feelings for your partner are very important.

Chapter 6

1. False. Willpower alone does not seem to help most men.

2. True. Almost all men under 30 years of age have quick ejaculation all or most of the time.

3. False. Orgasms for both men and women can range from mild to intense. It depends on the presence or absence of good and bad factors for sex at any given time.

4. False. It is more common for women than for men to feel fulfilled with sex without the need to have an orgasm. This does not mean that a woman will always be satisfied without an orgasm. It means that sometimes the woman does not need to have an orgasm to be satisfied.

5. True. A woman's physical makeup allows her to have many orgasms in a row. This does not mean that all women do. It simply means that women can have them. A woman's experience with sex and how aroused she is affect the number of orgasms she has.

Chapter 7

1. False. It is rather rare for men to have pain during intercourse. If a man has repeated pain, he should see a doctor.

2. False. Most of the time, pain during sex for women is linked to one or more factors. These can be medical factors, past trauma from sex, or negative messages about sex.

3. True. Over-the-counter lubricants can help most women with the lack of wetness. Also, for some women, hormone therapy can be helpful.

4. True.

5. True.

Chapter 8

1. False. Many factors can cause sex problems. A lack of love may affect sex, but it is not the most common factor that interferes with sex.

2. False. Most couples who take part in many kinds of sex activities besides intercourse enjoy sex more.

3. True. Talking often occurs at times of anger, so problems are often left unsolved.

4. False. It is not honesty or being direct that causes hurt feelings. Sarcasm and a lack of respect often do.

5. False. It is important to meet and feel at ease with a partner before having sex. So, single people with sex problems should socialize.

Chapter 9

1. False. It is not always possible to make sex what it was before. It is better for a couple to talk about realistic goals and to work toward those new goals. Realistic goals are crucial when age or health factors require a couple to adjust what they can expect from sex.

2. True. Setting aside time for you and your partner is always important. It helps create better conditions for being intimate. It also gives a strong message that the partnership is a priority.

3. False. There are many factors to consider before you have sex. The opportunity for sex only sets the stage. Other conditions, such as mood and feelings about sex, must also be present.

4. False. It never helps to blame each other even if one person brought a problem into a relationship. In most cases, both partners contribute equally to problems.

5. False. It is important to socialize and to find partners you feel at ease with. A partner you can talk openly and honestly with is the most important for solving a sex problem.

Chapter 10

1. False. The goal of therapy is for you to enjoy sex more and worry about sex less. Of course, making sex what it was before is possible. Most people do better by accepting a change in their sex life so that it is still enjoyable.

2. False. Planned sex and spontaneous sex can both be enjoyed. Most of the time, couples enjoy both.

3. False. A single person should look for a person who makes him or her feel at ease and not pressured about sex. Of course, there has to be some degree of sexual attraction, but it is not the most important factor.

4. True. Getting correct information is a first step in finding out what might be causing your problem.

5. True. Blaming another for a sex problem never helps. Most of the time, success in solving a sex problem comes from cooperating and not from blaming.

Chapter 11

1. True. Many sex problems stem from myths, lack of knowledge, or poor communication. Correct information has solved many sex problems. At the very least, it leads to success in solving a sex problem.

2. True. Much of the time, the fear of being criticized leads a person to avoid sex.

3. False. Most sex problems can be overcome in weeks or months, not years.

4. False. Therapists should always be neutral. Blame only gets in the way of progress.

5. False. There are two very good ways to find a therapist. One is to call a university and ask for the head of the psychiatry or psychology department. The other way is to call the state organization of the profession.

Chapter 12

1. True. Most of the time, knowledge about sex helps. A person is not likely to forget correct information about sex.

2. False. Everyone can expect to feel less comfort with sex at times. When such discomfort goes on for more than a few months, then it is time to seek help.

3. False. You should have sex as often as you and your partner want. Do not be guided by statistics or by what you think is expected.

4. True. For women, both the physical discomfort from childbirth and the new demands can interfere with sex. Men may also have less interest in sex because of the new demands.

5. True. For any change to occur, you must first want change to occur.

References

Buffum, J. (1982). Pharmacosexology: The effects of drugs on sexual function: A review. *Journal of Psychoactive Drugs, 14*(1–2), 5–44.

Carey, M., & Johnson, B. (in press). Effectiveness of yohimbine in the treatment of erectile disorder: Four meta-analytic integrations. *Archives of Sexual Behavior.*

Crooks, R., & Baur, K. (1993). *Our sexuality* (5th ed.). Redwood City, CA: Benjamin/Cummings.

Kinsey, A. C., Pomeroy, W. B., & Martin, C. E. (1948). *Sexual behavior in the human male.* Philadelphia: Saunders.

Laumann, E., Gagnon, J., Michael, R., & Michaels, S. (1994). *The social organization of sexuality: Sexual practices in the United States.* Chicago: University of Chicago Press.

McCarthy, B. W. (1988). *Male sexual awareness: Increasing sexual pleasure.* New York: Carroll & Graf.

Meston, C. M., & Gorzalka, B. B. (1992). Psychoactive drugs and human sexual behavior: The role of serotonergic activity. *Journal of Psychoactive Drugs, 24*(1), 1–40.

Rosen, R. C. (1991). Alcohol and drug effects on sexual response: Human experimental and clinical studies. *Annual Review of Sex Research, 2,* 119–179.

Rosen, R. C., & Ashton, A. K. (1993). Prosexual drugs: Empirical status of the "new aphrodisiacs." *Archives of Sexual Behavior, 22*(6), 521–543.

Wincze, J. P., & Carey, M. (1991). *Sexual dysfunction: A guide for assessment and treatment.* New York: Guilford Press.

Suggested Readings

Helpful Books

Crooks, R., & Baur, K. (1993). *Our sexuality* (5th ed.). Redwood City, CA: Benjamin/Cummings.

Laumann, E., Gagnon, J., Michael, R., & Michaels, S. (1994). *The social organization of sexuality: Sexual practices in the United States.* Chicago: University of Chicago Press.

Leiblum, S. R., & Rosen, R. C. (Eds.). (1989). *Principles and practice of sex therapy: Update for the 1990's* (2nd ed.). New York: Guilford Press.

McCarthy, B. W. (1988). *Male sexual awareness: Increasing sexual pleasure.* New York: Carroll & Graf.

Rosen, R. C., & Leiblum, S. R. (1992). *Erectile disorders: Assessment and treatment.* New York: Guilford Press.

Schover, L. R., & Jensen, S. B. (1988). *Sexuality and chronic illness: A comprehensive approach.* New York: Guilford Press.

Schover, L. R., & Randers–Pehrson, M. B. (1988). *Sexuality and cancer: For the man who has cancer and his partner.* New York: American Cancer Society.

Schover, L. R., & Randers–Pehrson, M. B. (1988). *Sexuality and cancer: For the woman who has cancer and her partner.* New York: American Cancer Society.

Spiess, W. F., Geer, J. H., & O'Donohue, W. T. (1984). Premature ejaculation: Investigation of factors in ejaculatory latency. *Journal of Abnormal Psychology, 93*(2), 242–245.

Wincze, J. P., & Carey, M. (1991). *Sexual dysfunction: A guide for assessment and treatment.* New York: Guilford Press.

Scientific Articles

Buffum, J. (1982). Pharmacosexology: The effects of drugs on sexual function. A review. *Journal of Psychoactive Drugs, 14*(1–2), 5–44.

Carey, M., & Johnson, B. (in press). Effectiveness of yohimbine in the treatment of erectile disorder: Four meta-analytic integrations. *Archives of Sexual Behavior.*

Kinsey, A. C., Pomeroy, W. B., & Martin, C. E. (1948). *Sexual behavior in the human male.* Philadelphia: Saunders.

Meston, C. M., & Gorzalka, B. B. (1992). Psychoactive drugs and human sexual behavior: The role of serotonergic activity. *Journal of Psychoactive Drugs, 24*(1), 1–40.

Rosen, R. C. (1991). Alcohol and drug effects on sexual response: Human experimental and clinical studies. *Annual Review of Sex Research, 2,* 119–179.

Rosen, R. C., & Ashton, A. K. (1993). Prosexual drugs: Empirical status of the "new aphrodisiacs." *Archives of Sexual Behavior, 22*(6), 521–543.

Spiess, W. F., Geer, J. H., & O'Donohue, W. T. (1984). Premature ejaculation: Investigation of factors in ejaculatory latency. *Journal of Abnormal Psychology, 93*(2), 242–245.

Wincze, J. P., Albert, A., & Bansal, S. (1993). Sexual arousal in diabetic females: Physiological and self-report measures. *Archives of Sexual Behavior, 22*(6), 587–601.